It's a Wonderful Life

Books by Ruskin Bond
Fiction
Miracle at Happy Bazaar: My Very Best Stories for Children
Rhododendrons in the Mist: My Favourite Tales of the Himalaya
A Gallery of Rascals: My Favourite Tales of Rogues, Rapscallions and Ne'er-do-wells
Unhurried Tales: My Favourite Novellas
Small Towns, Big Stories
Upon an Old Wall Dreaming
A Gathering of Friends
Tales of Fosterganj
The Room on the Roof & Vagrants in the Valley
The Night Train at Deoli and Other Stories
Time Stops at Shamli and Other Stories
Our Trees Still Grow in Dehra
A Season of Ghosts
When Darkness Falls and Other Stories
A Flight of Pigeons
Delhi is Not Far
A Face in the Dark and Other Hauntings
The Sensualist
A Handful of Nuts
Maharani
Secrets

Non-fiction
Rain in the Mountains
Scenes from a Writer's Life
Landour Days
Notes from a Small Room
The India I Love

Anthologies
A Town Called Dehra
Classic Ruskin Bond: Complete and Unabridged
Classic Ruskin Bond Volume 2: The Memoirs
Dust on the Mountain: Collected Stories
Friends in Small Places
Ghost Stories from the Raj
Great Stories for Children
Tales of the Open Road
The Essential Collection for Young Readers
Ruskin Bond's Book of Nature
Ruskin Bond's Book of Humour
The Writer on the Hill

Poetry
Hip-Hop Nature Boy & Other Poems
Ruskin Bond's Book of Verse

It's a Wonderful Life

ROADS TO HAPPINESS

Ruskin Bond

ALEPH BOOK COMPANY
An independent publishing firm
promoted by *Rupa Publications India*

First published in India in 2021
by Aleph Book Company
7/16 Ansari Road, Daryaganj
New Delhi 110 002

Copyright © Ruskin Bond 2021

Some essays and columns in the book have appeared in a slightly different form in *The Tribune* and *Times of India* and have been used with the permission of the author

All rights reserved.

The author has asserted his moral rights.

The views and opinions expressed in this book are those of the author and the facts are as reported by him, which have been verified to the extent possible, and the publisher is in no way liable for the same.

No part of this publication may be reproduced, transmitted, or stored in a retrieval system, in any form or by any means, without permission in writing from Aleph Book Company.

ISBN: 978-93-90652-40-2

7 9 10 8

Printed in India

This book is sold subject to the condition that it shall not, by way of trade or otherwise, be lent, resold, hired out, or otherwise circulated without the publisher's prior consent in any form of binding or cover other than that in which it is published.

Contents

Introduction: Breakfast with Ruskin / vii

The Writer From Jamnagar / 1

When All the Wars Are Done: Vignettes / 11

Never a Dull Moment: Essays / 31

It's a Wonderful Life: Lockdown Journals / 95

Introduction
Breakfast with Ruskin

By now, gentle reader, you will have assumed that my favourite meal is breakfast. An early morning cup of tea, an interlude of contemplation, and then a fried egg or an omelette with three hot, buttered toasts, one of them dripping with honey, all making a perfect start to what I hope will be a perfect day.

But it was not always so.

When I was a skinny nineteen-year-old, working in an office in London like a junior clerk in a Dickensian novel, I often had to go without breakfast. This was because I was always in a rush to catch the underground train in time, so that I would not arrive late at the said office, tucked away in a side-street off the Tottenham Court Road.

Charles Lamb, the great essayist, worked in a government office for many years and, like government servants the world over, did not keep regular hours.

'Late again, Mr Lamb,' admonished his office supervisor.

'True, sir,' countered Mr Lamb, 'But see how early I leave!'

So, I worked for a private firm, I did not have the privilege of coming and going at leisure. But that early morning dash, especially in mid-winter, meant that I had to sustain myself on a Marmite sandwich for the better part of the day.

But on Sundays, when I could get up at leisure, I would make myself a good breakfast—fried eggs and sausages, sometimes embellished with a kipper! I would even attempt the occasional omelette, experimenting with various ingredients, and sometimes the omelettes were too squishy or too flat or too spicy or too fluffy, undone or overdone, or just plain burnt, and I did seriously think of writing the cookbook to end all cookbooks, '101 Failed Omelettes and Other Disasters'.

But I finally managed to make an edible omelette, beaten up with just the right amount of chopped up green chillies, onion, garlic, and coriander. You could add the odd nasturtium leaf too, it will give it that little extra something.

Come, have breakfast with me. But if you shy away from nasturtium leaves, you can try this literary omelette of mine—essays and journal extracts beaten up with skits, sketches, reflections, memories, and words of wit if not of wisdom. Have it with your breakfast or use it as a bedside book. If nothing else, it will put you to sleep and banish all thoughts of dwindling bank balances, taxes falling due, COVID-19 concerns, and a polluted planet.

Nightmares crowd around us when we wake up. Then we must tackle the realities of daily life.

Start by breaking an egg.

Yes, break an egg at the break of day.

A good breakfast will chase the blues away.

Ruskin Bond
Landour
26 January 2021

The Writer From Jamnagar

'We are from Jamnagar,' said the head of the family of four who had come toiling up my steps on a cold but sunny Diwali morning. 'Our daughter has one of your books in school, and her teacher says you are the writer from Jamnagar! She would like to pay her respects.'

A smiling girl of about ten stepped forward and shook my hand. 'When were you in Jamnagar?' she asked.

'Eighty years ago,' I told her. 'The first six years of my life were spent there. That's where I learnt to read and write—in the little palace school.'

'That's why you're the writer from Jamnagar,' she said simply. 'And when will you come again?'

'Probably in my next life,' I said. 'It must be a very big city now; I wouldn't find the places I remember.'

'You'll find them,' she said.

Jamnagar! How quaint to be called 'the writer from Jamnagar'. I must say that it gave me a good feeling. I've grown used to being called 'the writer from Mussoorie', although there are a number of other writers who can lay their claim to that title. Jamnagar must have had other, mostly Gujarati, writers, to boast of, but in the years from 1934 to 1940, when I was an infant and then a troublesome small boy, the only 'writer' we knew of was Mrs Ghosh, the secretary to Jam Sahib, the state's ruler. Mrs Ghosh was always to be found before Jam Sahib's desk, taking dictation and writing letters to potentates all over the world.

Jamnagar was a small state with a small port and a very rich maharaja, or Jam Sahib as he was called. He owned dozens of Rolls-Royces and an equal number of chauffeurs. He was also a very generous man who, when World War II broke out, gave refuge to several thousand Polish families fleeing from Hitler's storm troopers.

Jamnagar was also the state where Indian cricket was born. So the earlier ruler, Ranjit Sinhji, played for England; a magnificent batsman; so did his nephew, Duleep Sinhji, a master of the glide to leg. And it was on the Jamnagar ground that the great all-rounder Vinoo Mankad won his spurs, going on to make a double century at Lord's, a few years later.

I have memories of the cricket ground in Jamnagar, although not of the cricket. Sitting with my parents in the VIP section, my attention was given over to the steady rotation of trays of sweets—gulab jamuns, rasgullas, jalebis, barfis, savouries of every kind—that circulated among the spectators. How could a small boy concentrate on the cricket when all these delicacies kept finding their way into his greedy little hands. No wonder, then, that when I did grow up to play a little cricket, I was inevitably made the twelfth man, carrying out the drinks and refreshments for the rest of the team.

So, what were we doing in Jamnagar just before the war and Indian Independence?

My father was a travelling teacher who, rather than teach

in a school, preferred to take up tutorial jobs in the Indian states, of which there were many in those days. He had taught young princes in Bharatpur and Alwar, and at the time of my birth he had moved to the Kathiawar states, doing stints in Jatpur and Pithodia before starting a small palace school in Jamnagar, where we were to live till 1941.

It was a small school, occupying one large room in an old palace, and most of the pupils were girls. I remember them clearly (and still have their photographs): Mamta, who was the oldest, about twelve, and quite beautiful; Janak, who was chubby and jolly, always pinching my cheeks; Ratna, serious, thoughtful; and 'Hathi', my age, very sweet and mischievous. These were all princesses. There was also the little prince, the heir to the throne, but I did not see much of him, he was being groomed for a public school, I think. But I do have a photograph of the two of us romping in the sea of Balachadi beach.

The old palace had a turret going up two or three floors, and at the top was a small glassed-in room, each pane of glass a different colour. This was my favourite place. I loved looking through those coloured panes, at the lake or the main palace or the gardens, tinted pink or blue or green or purple or orange. Many years later, I was to write a story centred around this room. It was called 'The Room of Many Colours'. In the story there was an eccentric Rani who gave me sweets, but she was a figment of my imagination. Many of my stories are like that. I start by describing a known place, or persons, and then my imagination takes over and the incidents run away from me.

But this is a memoir, so I must tell the truth.

We had a good cook, but he was not the one who cooked for Jim Corbett while the great hunter was felling man-eating tigers. Our cook made excellent fish cutlets and guava jam, and he ran away with the ayah; but those were the only accomplishments that I can recall.

I should have said that my ayah ran away with the cook, for she was the stronger personality. She reigned supreme in the house. My father never punished me. My mother tried to, but I was too elusive. But there was no escaping ayah's large hands if she was on the warpath. She wouldn't hesitate to bend me over her knee and smack me hard on the bottom. She was fond of me, and in a way, it was a sign of ownership, for she knew no one else would go so far as to give me a good spanking.

I was a funny child. I loved sweeping the veranda steps. I had watched the ayah doing this occasionally, so I borrowed her broom and swept the steps and the veranda whenever they grew muddy or covered with fallen leaves. It gave me a passion for tidiness. I don't sweep verandas any more (just in case you want to hire me for the job), but I like a neat house and my books and papers in the right place. Like Hercule Poirot, if a picture on the wall isn't hanging properly, I'll straighten it.

But I hated haircuts. I dreaded the monthly visits of the unfortunate man who had to cut my hair. I would go into hiding, and when found, would have to be rolled up in a bedsheet and taken, kicking and screaming, to a high chair where my golden locks would be shorn off. On one occasion my mother lost patience with me and let me go halfway through the haircut. For weeks, I went about looking like a cartoon-strip character, long hair on one side of my head and short hair on the other. Today, it would be considered the height of fashion!

I was a nervous, sensitive child. Jamnagar had a small airfield, and one of the princes offered to take my mother and I on a spin in a Tiger Moth, one of those double-winged planes that were then the latest thing in tourist aviation. It was a two-seater, and my mother got me behind the pilot and tried to get me to join her. But I was suddenly overcome with fear. I panicked, and fled from the airfield.

On another occasion, my father took me aboard a dhow, a large sailing vessel that plied across the Gulf of Kutch. It rolled and pitched so much that I demanded to be taken off. I made such a scene that the ship's crew were only too glad to put me ashore, much to the embarrassment of my poor father.

It was a small port with a couple of landing points—Bedi Bunder and Rosi Bunder. A long causeway went a considerable distance into the sea, and I enjoyed walking up and down this causeway with my parents, watching the seagulls and the fishing boats; but nothing could persuade me to get into a boat.

A small steamer sometimes called at the port, and its captain, a jolly Scotsman, came over to dinner and jokingly offered to take me on a long voyage around the world—Yokohama, San Diego, London. Somehow, I didn't see myself swabbing the deck like Jim Hawkins in *Treasure Island*, but I promised to join him one day. Years later, I put him in an early short story, 'Faraway Places', and called him Captain MacWhirr after the captain in Joseph Conrad's *Typhoon*, one of my favourite stories. But our little tramp steamer would never have stood up to a typhoon; it seemed content to ply up and down the Malabar coast.

I have mentioned *Treasure Island*. There was no bookshop in Jamnagar, and no library that I can recall, and my father's classroom had only a few simple English books. But at home there was a big book of nursery rhymes, and old and well-thumbed copies of *Treasure Island* and *Alice in Wonderland*. And as soon as I could read by myself (without my father's help), I was devouring these books, reading them twice over for want of anything else to read. It was only when we left Jamnagar that I had access to a wider selection of books; and then, hungry for the written word, I would read almost anything that came my way.

There were, of course, comic papers that came my way. Country Commander Bourne's teenage son had them sent out to him from England: *The Dandy*, *The Beano*, *Comic Cuts*, *The Wizard*, and *Magnet* with its stories of Billy Bunter the fat boy of Greyfriars School. Some of these were story papers, not simple cartoon strips.

Commander Bourne was the state's port authority. He was a genial, hospitable man. Tragically, he developed gangrene due to an injury to his foot. One amputation led to another, but he succumbed to spreading infection. Those were the days before penicillin, and the other antibiotics had not been discovered yet.

Our basic home remedy was 'pinky', crystals of potassium permanganate. When I was badly stung by bees (having disturbed their nest on the steps to the roof of our bungalow), my father bathed my wounds (on my arms and legs) with a solution of 'pinky', and it brought some relief. But the adventure with the beehive taught me to admire nature without interfering with it.

At first, I was afraid of the turkeys in the state farm. 'Gobble-gobble-gobble,' they called, as they clustered around Mr Jenkins at feeding time—their red wattles and pendulous dewlaps were quite alarming at first. But they were a friendly lot, and they had more 'character' than hens and ducks. The geese were quite aggressive, and I gave them a wide berth.

Mr and Mrs Jenkins were a Welsh couple who ran the farm. If I dropped in on them, I could always expect a home-made lemonade and ginger biscuit.

The Jam Sahib employed a number of Europeans and was always very good to their families. My little sister and I were the recipients of numerous toys, dolls, trainsets, teddy bears, Diwali crackers, Christmas puddings.... And there was a car at our disposal. Not a Rolls-Royce, but a sturdy Hillman which opened at the top; ideal for evening drives into the countryside or along the coast.

But most evenings, I sat with my father at the dining table, helping him to sort and arrange his impressive stamp collection. He had albums for different countries, and he arranged and mounted his stamps in sets, according to their date of issue. There were rare stamps from the early days of the Indian and world postal systems, and there were also colourful new issues from small islands and emerging nations. He would deal with philatelists and stamp dealers in Bombay and London, and the well-known Stanley Gibbons catalogues were always at hand. The table had to be cleared for dinner, and sometimes dinner would be late; we were so absorbed in making the albums attractive. My mother wasn't interested in stamps, but she put up with these sessions because they kept me out of mischief.

'One day these albums will be yours,' my father told me, 'so you must know everything about them, especially valuable rarities.'

But when he died in Calcutta five years later, the entire collection vanished mysteriously. But that's another story.

The Jamnagar period was a good time for us. My parents were still in the early years of their marriage, and there was no indication that it was going to break up.

We had a wind-up gramophone and a box full of 78 rpm records. There were nursery rhymes on one of the records, and one of the rhymes went something like this:

> Oh, what have you got
> For dinner, Mrs Bond?
> There are geese in the parlour
> And ducks in the pond.

Mrs Bond did not have to worry about making dinner, but she enjoyed making pickles, chutneys, and sauces, and these were usually tested on me before being bottled and preserved. As a result, I became, in time, a collector of pickles. Unlike stamps, they disappear only in one direction. From jackfruits to bitter gourds to sweet lemons to plums, I have had my share of pickles and chutneys, and they still decorate my shelves and dining table.

While my mother was making pickles, and my father was teaching the princesses to read and write, I would be winding up the gramophone, changing the needle and the record, and playing anything from music-hall comic songs to grand opera. My father had a liking for opera, and I listened to it, too, enchanted by the big booming voices of tenors and baritones—Caruso, Chaliapin, Gigli, Tauber. Puccini's operas were very romantic, and some of those lovely arias still linger in my memory. '*Che gehda manina.... se la lasci riscaldar*'. Your tiny hand is frozen, let me warm it into life!

Hard to imagine a frozen hand in the heat and humidity of Jamnagar, but *La Bohème* and *Madame Butterfly* were my favourites. And the light operas or operettas (now out of fashion) gave us many romantic melodies: Nelson Eddy singing 'Softly, As In the Morning Sunrise', Richard Crooks singing 'Only a Rose', John McCormack singing, 'The Mountains of Mourne'.

Over the years, I have missed those golden voices, but last month little Shrishti searched on her mobile app, and there they all were, resurrected for my benefit! For a couple of hours, I wallowed in musical nostalgia. Technology has its merits.

'Romance brought up the nine-fifteen!' wrote Kipling, and it was the nine-fifteen that took us from Jamnagar to Dehradun, a journey of three days (with changes along the way) in those distant times.

Hitler was rampaging all over Europe, and Britain declared war on Germany. The Japanese army was about to swarm all over Asia, even up to the doors of India. My father felt it was his duty to 'join up', as the expression went, and the Jam Sahib, who supported the Allied war effort, encouraged him to do so.

My father was then in his forties, too old for active service, but he was taken into the Codes and Ciphers section of the RAF. It was the kind of work that suited his temperament.

He joined Air Headquarters in New Delhi (where I was to join him two years later), and my mother, sister, and I went to live with my grandmother in Dehradun. My parents' marriage began to break up soon after, and the outcome was a very turbulent period in my life. It's a story I have told elsewhere.

I did not see Jamnagar again. It's a big industrial city now, I'm told. My memories are of spacious lawns and palaces, small steamers and lonely beaches, and a room with windowpanes of different colours. This childhood helped me to become a writer; so truly, I am a writer from Jamnagar.

Today, eighty years on, it all seems another lifetime.

But I can't help wondering.... What happened to all those turkeys?

WHEN ALL THE WARS ARE DONE

Vignettes

Paddle Your Own Canoe

Towards the end of the school term I was told, very gently, by one of the school masters, that my father was no more; that he had gone to heaven, because God had important work for him.

I was only ten, and it seemed to me that God had been unreasonable in requiring my father's services at a time when I needed him more than anyone else; but I was to learn in order to get through life without too much heartbreak, it was better not to depend too much on favours from above. 'Paddle your own canoe', were the words he had inscribed in my autograph album, and I decided to do just that, although I was to make a rather clumsy rower, with the canoe just about managing to stay afloat down the river for many years.

Rubber Plant

My rubber plant. About the only plant that has flourished in this room over a period of time. Geraniums and begonias give up after a season or two. But not the rubber plant. Its tendrils find a bit of wall to cling to, the leaves spread out, the tough stem travels slowly but surely along the wall, heading towards my bed. Is it going to strangle me one day, or does it just want to make love? Both, perhaps.

There is definitely something erotic about rubber plants. See how their glossy, oblong dark green leaves emerge from an orange-red sheath. *Ficus elastica* to give its botanical name. There are other members of the fig family, but this one—the decora variety—likes my bedroom. And it's making for my bed!

Wheels

The little Buddhist prayer wheel near my window revolves in the morning sunshine. It reminds me of how dependent we are on wheels. Originally bullock-cart wheels and horse-drawn carts and chariots. Then bicycles and buses and trains and motor cars and fast bikes. Even planes need wheels for landing and taking off. My watch runs on a little wheel. So many things open and close at the turn of a wheel. A ship doesn't run on wheels, but the captain is at the wheel to steer it safely on its way.

I suppose computers can do a lot of things that wheels used to do.

Not so long ago, I watched a couple of fishermen paddling a small canoe into the surging waters of the Bay of Bengal. No wheels, no computer! And it reminded me of something my father used to say: 'Paddle your own canoe!' Do your own thing, don't depend too much on others.

Paddle your own canoe. And if you sink, you only have yourself to blame.

Impatient Wind

It was a still morning, but now the wind is about, swirling around the house, humming to itself, and whistling, and grumbling a little as it rattles at the windows.

Impatient wind! It is always trying to get somewhere. How like a human being—anxious to arrive; ambitious; wanting to dominate. But in the end getting nowhere, just dying out as it loses itself across the wide, unending plains.

'Listen to me, listen to me!' it seems to say, as it struggles against the windowpane.

I am listening, but like an empty speech it has nothing to say. Wordless, it leaves, and the besieged swallow returns to its nest in the eaves.

The Sound of Silence

Car horns on the road. You can get used to them after some time.

Bikes revving up. Not so easy to get used to, but you grin and bear it.

A truck rumbles past, an ambulance turns on its siren. All par for the course.

A crow arrives at the window. Caw, caw, caw! Shut up, crow, what are you doing here?

Night comes on. All is peaceful, all is still. Just listen to the silence!

Sexy Earthworms

Earthworms, I've just learnt, have a great sex life. In fact, they are at it almost all the time, lovingly entwined in each other's coils. And they are bisexual too, which saves time.

Earthworms are, of course, great tillers of the soil, and without them our plants and crops would wither away.

So the next time I'm turning up the soil in a flowerpot, and come across a couple of earthworms, I won't throw them out, as in former times. I shall return them to Mother Earth with my blessings. 'Have a good time, little ones. And may you have hundreds of baby worms to keep our planet healthy, wealthy, and wise.'

I suppose there's something to be said for living underground. Although, personally, I would rather live above ground.

Alice in Wonderland was, at first, titled 'Alice's Adventures Underground', but Lewis Carroll very wisely changed the title. Readers did not want to be reminded 'of graves and worms and epitaphs'.

But those earthworms do a better job than any chemical or fertilizer. Let's wish them a happy life.

Room With a View

With only occasional breaks, I have lived in this room for over thirty-six years, and it hasn't changed much in that time. In the early years, the roof used to blow off in a storm, and on one occasion, I woke up to find a sheet of snow on my blanket. Rakesh was still a schoolboy at the time and thought it was great fun.

In recent years, Rakesh and Beena have strengthened the walls, roof, and ceiling, and cold winds are content to whistle around the veranda. Still, it's a very old building and catches the brunt of the elements. But it's been standing for well over a hundred years, and hopefully will survive a little longer, though it does tremble a bit when the traffic is heavy.

No sign of ivy on the walls of Ivy Cottage, but on looking up the records I discovered that the building was at first called 'Eva Cottage'. The name was changed around 1920. When the ownership changed.

What does grow on the walls, flowering all summer, is the sorrel (also known as Almora grass) which flourishes on limestone walls and cliffs. Clusters of little pink flowers bloom like confetti. At school, when we were hungry, we would eat the sweet-and-sour flowers. Too many, and you'd be running to the toilet.

A Postal Relic

Going through an old trunk, I came across my postal savings passbook, a relic of my sojourn in London over sixty years ago. Address: Haverstock Hill, NW3. Balance: five shillings, six pence. I wonder if I could claim some interest on that amount!

My weekly wage in 1953 was a little over five pounds after the deduction of the National Insurance (which enabled me to spend a month in Hampstead General Hospital at government expense), and out of this, I was able to save about five shillings every week. The rest went on food, my bed-sitting room, and occasional evenings at the theatre or cinema. I worked as an accounts clerk, wrote my first novel at night, and when I had saved fifty pounds I came back to India aboard the MS *Batory*, a Polish liner. There had been a mutiny on board and some of the crew had deserted, so there was a reduction in the fare to Bombay. In the Red Sea, a passenger fell overboard and drowned. An astrologer returning to India. The seas foretold what the stars could not foretell.

All this comes back to me when I look at this well-thumbed old postal passbook. 5sh. 6p. That's how I saw *Porgy and Bess*, with the beautiful Leontyne Price singing 'Summertime'.

Summertime

Summertime in India. Summertime is mango time. It is also the time when the hot winds blow in from the desert, filling your New Delhi bungalow with a coating of dust.

You have protection now, but when I was a boy there was no air conditioning and you kept cool by hanging a khas-khas mat over the front door and drenching it with water every now and then. The bhisti did this for you, carrying cool water in his goatskin bag.

In the villages, you sought the cool shade of peepul or banyan trees. The heart-shaped peepul leaf, its slender waist compared to Lord Krishna's, revolves in the slightest breeze. And when all the leaves are moving, rustling in the faintest puff of wind, the mind and body are rested and refreshed.

In the hills, summertime for me meant a woodpecker knocking away at an old oak tree, and wild dog roses flowering on the bank of a mountain stream.

Old Oak Tree

It is over two hundred years old, which means it was here before the hill station came up. The oaks and rhododendrons are indigenous to this area; the pines take over a little higher up; the deodars like the cool north face of the mountain.

The oak tree saw the first house come up; saw the red-coat soldiers come and go; saw traders from the plains open their shops, selling to the white folk, selling to the men and women from the surrounding villages who came to the market, the women in their colourful flounced skirts. A British settler would marry a pretty village girl. Families came up from the plains to escape the heat. Schools opened. The town changed, but the villages remained the same—cut off, neglected.

The old oak tree has seen all this and more. Hopefully it will still be here, fifty years from now, giving shelter to curious tourists. A pity it could not record all the events it has witnessed.

Purple Pansy

A pansy! February is not the season for flowers, but Beena brings me this potted pansy from a nursery in Dehra.

There was a time when delicate or effeminate young men were called pansies, for no good reason. The pansy is a sturdy little plant with many coloured blooms. Its cheerful round countenance always reminds me of the face of that wonderful comedian, Oliver Hardy who, with his partner, Stan Laurel, gave cinemagoers so much pleasure.

This particular pansy, now in occupation of my sunny window ledge, is a deep purple.

Purple is a colour that always went with royalty (as well as with jamuns, a royal fruit) and this is certainly a royal pansy.

Connections

No trains up here, but down in the valley, last week, I heard the distant whistle of a train.

It took me back to my childhood when, roaming the outskirts of Dehra, I would stop to watch a train rushing past. Sometimes I would wave to the passengers, or rather, to those who were at the windows, and sometimes they would wave back. We would never meet; but for an instant, a fleeting instant, there would be a connection between the waving boy and passing traveller, and these connections made the world less lonely.

Sometimes, in my dreams, I see those trains again, only now they are rushing through the sky.

Spring

Spring is here, and in the hills the plum, apricot, and apple trees are in blossom. The pale pink of the apricot vies with the creamy white of the plum. A hailstorm and the fallen blossoms mingle on the hillside. But enough have survived to give us summer fruit.

Down in the valley and all across the plains, a heady fragrance assails the traveller. The mango trees are in blossom. How I love their aroma!

Another month, and the ripening fruit will be attracting flocks of parrots and other lovers of the golden fruit. Small creatures love it while it's still green.

But where have all the parrots gone? Like so many birds, they seem to be on the decline.

The Sewing Machine

Listening to the hum and rattle of a sewing machine in the front room, I realize that there are many things that haven't changed much in a hundred years.

The sewing machine, for example. And the large pair of scissors beside it. And the tailor himself, a bearded old man full of courteous conversation, he hasn't changed. He sits on the carpeted floor all day, making sofa covers. And sofa covers haven't changed much, either!

The Horse Chestnut Tree

The horse chestnut tree always has something to offer. Early in April, it produces those handsome candelabras of pink and white blossom, then tender green leaves, turned darker as the year progresses. Then the chestnuts appear, and by autumn they are bursting through their jackets and falling to the ground. Shiny brown chestnuts. And by November, the leaves have turned yellow, decorating the footpaths as they float slowly to the ground. I love handling chestnuts. Sometimes I keep one in my pocket, just for luck.

The Last Leopard and Other Vignettes

Bright red
The poinsettia flames,
 As autumn and the old year wanes

˜

New moon in a deep purple sky.

˜

Returning to Mussoorie from Rajpur around midnight, we saw a leopard leap over a parapet wall, then her three cubs scurrying into the bushes. I had thought I'd seen my last leopard some years ago. But there they were—a family of survivors.

˜

I'm watching the stars from my window. Every time I do this, I am aware of belonging to the universe rather than to just one corner of the earth.

˜

The first really warm day of the year. I could feel the sap rising in every limb. I forgot my sore knee and did a little jig. Then looked around to see if anyone was watching. Only the ginger cat on the roof across the road. He was watching me very intently, wondering what I was up to.

∽

Another sign of summer's approach: a ladybird walked across the papers on my desk. I held out my hand and it crawled on to my palm. A bit ticklish. So, I deposited it on a leaf of the rubber plant. It seems quite happy there.

∽

Dark clouds approach. Thunder blossoms in the air. I close the window. Lightning streaks across the opposite hill—Pari Tibba, Hill of the Fairies. I'm sure the fairies would have taken shelter underground, or in the trunks of old oak trees.

∽

This day I heard the whistling thrush, its sweet, old song.

There's a pair of them, making a nest in the old retaining wall behind the house. It's shady there, cool and private. I think I'll give them my 'Do Not Disturb' placard that hangs on the front door. No one pays any attention to it.

∽

I love to see seeds sprouting and coming up where I have planted them, even if they are only chillies and beans. Those tender green shoots are the basic miracle of life.

And I suppose the chilli is the true emblem of India. It keeps everyone on the hop.

There are chairs and there are chairs, but as we grow older, we gravitate towards a particular chair, one that has grown accustomed to us and to our figure. My own favourite is an old cane chair that has been around for many years. It has taken the shape of my bottom; either that, or my bottom has taken the shape of the chair. What is certain is that there is more of the author than there used to be.

And, when all the wars are done, a butterfly will still be beautiful.

I wrote this line a few years ago, after a conflict in which a number of people lost their lives.

Today, there are many more conflicts, all over the world, and they appear to be building up into a major conflagration. But when a plain white butterfly appeared on my windowsill, heralding the summer, I had to admit that there is still some beauty in the world.

NEVER A DULL MOMENT

Essays

The Horseshoe

'What's this?' asked Rakesh when he was a small boy, touching the huge horseshoe that stood on my desk.

'It's a horseshoe,' I said. 'I keep it for luck.'

'But it's so big! It must have been a very big horse. Like a dinosaur!'

'Not a dinosaur, but an English carthorse. They are not very tall, but they are sturdy animals, used to pull carts and ploughs. And they have big feet. About four times bigger than the feet of the little hill ponies we see in Mussoorie.'

'Are there any carthorses in India?'

'Not as far as I know. You'll find them on farms in England or France.'

'Then how did you get it, Dada?'

'Miss Bean gave it to me.'

And then I told Rakesh about Miss Bean, the old English lady who had grown up in Mussoorie, and who lived in Maplewood Cottage when I came to live there in 1963.

Yes, it's exactly fifty years since I came to live in the hill station, renting the little cottage that stood on its own on the edge of a maple and oak forest. Rakesh wasn't born then.

Miss Bean was in her eighties, the 'last surviving Bean' as she described herself. Her parents, brother, and sister were all buried in the Camel's Back cemetery. She received a tiny pension and lived in a small room full of bric-a-brac, bits of furniture rescued from her old home, and paintings done by her late mother. I was on my own then, living on sardines, baked beans, and other tinned stuff. Sometimes, I shared my simple meals with her.

She told me stories of Mussoorie's early days—the balls and fancy dress parties at Hakman's & the Savoy; the scandals that erupted from time to time; houses that were said to be haunted; friends who had gone away or gone to their Maker; her father's military exploits.

I had noticed the big horseshoe on the mantelpiece and asked her how she came by it. 'It was supposed to bring me luck. But the good luck ran out long ago.... You can have it, if you like it.' And she presented me with the horseshoe.

Well, it's been with me all these years, going almost unnoticed most of the time, except when a visitor notices it and comments on its size.

Miss Bean passed away in her sleep while I was still at Maplewood. Prem came to work for me, and brought his wife and three-month old Rakesh from the village to live with us. They stayed for the rest of my long sojourn in the hills.

Rakesh is now forty. He and his pretty wife, Beena, have three schoolgoing children. The horseshoe is still reclining on my desk.

Beena was asking me about it this morning. 'Did it really bring you good luck?'

'We make our own luck,' I said. 'But that horseshoe has been with us all these years, and it always reminds me of its former owner, a kind old lady who didn't have much luck, but who enjoyed living, and stood alone, without complaining. It's courage, not luck, that takes us through to the end of the road.'

Miss Bean had the courage to stand alone. And she lives on through that old horseshoe on my desk.

Every Night, Before I Sleep

Every night, before I sleep, I spend at least ten to fifteen minutes reading some great poetry. It may be Wordsworth or Keats, Robert Frost or Rabindranath Tagore, or some poem chosen at random, and I always find that this little indulgence helps me to enjoy a good night's sleep.

There is nothing more detrimental to sleep than watching television late at night. There was a time when I felt I had to keep up with the latest news, national or global, before going to bed; but this has become increasingly depressing, and I now find it difficult to sleep if I am haunted by images of starving children in Syria, or mobs on the rampage at our railway stations, or universities in turmoil, or psychopaths gunning down innocent people at random in America, or terrorists doing more of the same, and bombs and other weapons becoming bigger and deadlier.

It is not as though the poets were immune to all of this. On the contrary, they got to the crux of the matter, as Matthew Arnold did in *Dover Beach*:

> Ah, love, let us be true
> To one another! for the world, which seems
> To lie before us like a land of dreams,

> So various, so beautiful, so new,
> Hath really neither joy, nor love, nor light,
> Nor certitude, nor peace, nor help for pain;
> And we are here as on a darkling plain
> Swept with confused alarms of struggle and flight,
> Where ignorant armies clash by night.

I think that last line says it all, and the poem is even more relevant today than when it was written a hundred and fifty years ago. A television screen late at night can bring those ignorant armies right into your bedroom, and prevent you from sleeping.

I used to turn to televised debates for some relief. Would they provide me some intellectual stimulation before I turned the lights off? Alas, no. Unlike a civilized school debate, these televised debates on national issues are often hostile confrontations, and in a short time the participants are shouting and screaming at each other and bandying insults, and they are paid for doing it, too!

I turn to the sports channel.

I should have stopped at the badminton or golf, both civilized sports. But, egged on by Gautam, my twelve-year-old grandson, I find myself watching an extraordinary wrestling tournament in which a couple of overdeveloped hulks are stamping on each other, doing their best to break each other's necks or arms, punching and butting, all without apparently inflicting serious injury.

'It's all acting,' my knowledgeable grandson informs me. 'They rehearse in advance.'

I take his word for it, and move to the next channel,

which is anything but a well-rehearsed wrestling match. This is kick-boxing with a vengeance, although the fists, only lightly gloved, do most of the damage. By the end of the bout, the loser's face is a bloody mess. You don't want to go to bed with a vision of a face beaten to a pulp. You will see it all night and dream of a large fist smashing into your face.

But fisticuffs are the in-thing, it seems. Only the other day, a certain Donald Trump, leading Republican candidate[*] for the US presidency, threatened to punch a protestor in the face. Obviously, he grew up on John Wayne movies.

I grew up on movies, too, although my preference was for Gene Kelly, singing and dancing in the rain, or the Marx Brothers creating mayhem at the circus or opera. So, I use my remote to turn to the movie channels available on our TV set.

'Only action movies today,' says Gautam in anticipation.

But it's more than action, it's pure torture in every sense of the word.

Here is some madman's victim being skinned alive. Move on. Now someone is having his eyes gouged out. Move on quickly. Another victim is having his legs sawn off. Madmen abound! So do aliens and anacondas. Some poor woman is being swallowed, head first, by a giant anaconda. And if you don't care for anacondas you can switch to the next channel and watch a group of scantily clad bathers being snapped up by hungry crocodiles. No doubt they taste better without their clothes on.

Finally, I switch off the TV and drink a cup of cocoa to calm my nerves. A hot rum would help, but suddenly

---

[*]This was written before Trump's election to the presidency.

Old Monk has gone off the market and I am not a whisky drinker. But there is always poetry—and the stars outside.

I send Gautam to bed. No more anacondas or kick-boxers for him. I go to my window and look out into the night. The moon is coming up over Landour, and a deodar on the summit stands out in silhouette. Far down in the valley the lights of the Doon twinkle up at me. An owl hoots gently, and a flying squirrel glides from one treetop to another.

Some lines from a favourite poet, Walter de la Mare, come back to me:

> Look thy last on all things lovely,
> Every hour. Let no night
> Seal thy sense in deathly slumber
> Till to delight
> Thou have paid thy utmost blessing....

Yes, this is the hour for poetry, a time to remind oneself that there is still beauty in the world, and that sleep comes best to those who look for the beautiful in thought and words before turning in for the night.

If you would dream of dragonflies instead of dragons, then turn off that mind-disturbing TV set, turn on that bed light, and give yourself up to a few words of enchantment. Try Robert Herrick, that most gentle of poets, as he speaks to his beloved:

> I dare not ask to kiss,
> I dare not beg a smile,
> Lest having that, or this,
> I might grow proud the while.

> No, no, the utmost share
> Of my desire shall be
> Only to kiss the air
> That lately kissed thee.

And with this most tender of kisses, I say goodnight to you, dear reader.

Some Insect Friends—and Foes

Now that the rains are here, the house spiders emerge from their homes to enjoy the moist, cool air. Folklore tells us that when a spider runs up the wall, the rain is going to fall. And, when it runs down the wall, the house is going to fall!

My particular spider can't make up its mind. Sometimes it's running up the wall, sometimes it's scurrying down the wall. Maybe it's just looking for a mate. Monsoon time is mating time! But when a female spider has finished mating, she loses no time feasting on her helpless husband.

Gautam reminds me that spiders are not really insects. Spiders have eight legs while true insects—such as beetles, butterflies, and bugs of all kinds—have six.

Actually, my spider has seven legs, probably having lost one while getting rid of her husband. She's like Susanna in *7 Khoon Maaf*.

Talking of bugs, there was this beautiful little beetle that sailed into my room last evening. It was about twice the size of a ladybird, and it had a beautiful green sheen, just like an emerald. Some beetles, especially the smaller ones, are really beautiful to behold. They come in many colours and patterns—nature's true gems.

Up here at Ivy Cottage, it's very open and windy, and I don't see many of the larger beetles. But when I lived at Maplewood, near the forest, I would often be visited by those giants of the insect world—bamboo, rhino, and stag beetles—who, attracted by the light from my sitting room, would fly in at the open window and usually land—with a splash—in my goldfish bowl.

The goldfish, always well-behaved, would show no sign of resentment at these intrusions; but I had to save the beetles from drowning, and I would rescue them from a watery end and send them into the night again.

I like goldfish. They are the perfect companions. They don't bark, roar, growl, howl, grunt, shriek, or make a mess on the carpet. They don't bite, unless they happen to be piranhas. I can dress or undress in front of a goldfish without feeling embarrassed.

And they show no signs of being embarrassed either.

I can't say the same about other creatures.

The other day, when I was getting out of my pyjamas (and hopefully into my trousers), a large rhesus monkey appeared at the window and bared her teeth in a most ferocious manner. Was it exhibiting fury, or just plain mirth? To an animal, the human body must look quite ridiculous; and I foresee the time when we'll be the ones in cages, and the animals will be on the outside, grinning at us.

Well, all my monkey wanted was a banana, so I gave her one, just to wipe the grin off her face. And away she went, telling her friends all about my purple pyjamas.

⌒

Butterflies are beautiful, beetles are pearlescent, and dragonflies catch fire in the sun, but I draw the line at houseflies, who are utterly devoid of charm or good manners.

Yesterday, there was this large fly buzzing against the windowpane, anxious to get out. Good-hearted as ever, I opened the window, allowed him to make his escape, then closed the window again. Barely a minute later he was back, buzz-buzz-buzz, let me out, let me out! How on earth did he get in? There must be a secret passage.

'Once more into the breach!' I recalled King Henry V's speech before the Battle of Agincourt (studied in Class 9), and dashed to the rescue again.

Exit the fly. I'm back at my desk, trying to look like Wordsworth. Buzz-buzz-buzz, it's that fly again.

The charge of the Light Brigade. 'Into the valley of death rode the six hundred!' Exit the fly! Back to my love lyric. Buzz-buzz-buzz!

Rungli-Rungliot. 'Thus far and no further....'

I fold my *Times of India* and give the fly a mighty thump, ending its existence. The print media can still make a difference.

I return to my desk, flexing my muscles, feeling all-powerful like Donald Trump.

Buzz-buzz-buzz!

There are now *two* flies at the window, trying to get out. Or summoning their relatives.

No matter how smart we think we are, nature always has the last laugh.

A New Horn

As the taxi weaved its way in and out of the Meerut traffic and headed for Delhi, Gurbachan Singh took his hand off the horn and gave me a brief, triumphant look.

'What do you think of my horn?' he asked.

'Oh, it's a fine horn,' I said, wringing out my ears. 'It couldn't be louder.'

'You can hear it half a mile ahead,' said Gurbachan proudly, as he blasted off at two young men who were sharing a bicycle. They moved out of the way with alacrity.

'It makes a lot of noise in the car, too,' I said, and added hastily, 'Not that I object, you know....'

'Doesn't your horn have more than one tone of voice?' asked a fellow traveller with a trace of irritation.

'Two!' claimed Gurbachan. 'Male and female. Just see!' And then he produced a high note and then a low note on the horn, both equally ear-shattering. Ahead of us, a tonga ran off the road and on to the cart track.

'This is one terrific horn,' said Gurbachan. 'I have had it made especially for this taxi. No foreign horns for me. They are not loud enough. Indian horns are the best.'

'Indian noise is the best,' said the fellow traveller.

In an interval of comparative quiet, I found myself

reflecting on the nature of sound—the unpleasantness of some sounds, and the sweetness of others, and why certain sounds (like motor horns) can be sweet to some and hideous to others. The sweetest sound of all, I decided, was silence. There are many kinds of silence—the silence of an empty room, the silence of the mountains, the silence of prayer, or the enforced silence of loneliness—but the best kind of silence, I concluded, was the silence that comes after the cessation of noise.

'It was made in the Jama Masjid area,' continued Gurbachan, interrupting my thoughts. 'Seventy-five rupees only. Made by hand, to my own specifications. There's only one drawback—it must not get wet!'

As his hand settled down on the horn again, I thought of praying for rain, but the sky being clear and blue I decided that a prayer would be an unreasonable demand on the Creator.

'Ah, but you don't know what it is to have a horn like this one. Try it, sir. Why don't you try it for yourself?'

'Oh, that's all right,' I assured him. 'You have proved its excellence already.'

'No, you must try it. I insist that you try it!' He was like a big boy, suddenly generous, determined on sharing a new toy with a younger brother.

He grabbed my hand and placed it on the horn; and as I felt it give a little, a thrill of pleasure rushed up my arm. I pressed hard, and a stream of music flowed in and out of the car. Now I could understand the happiness and the supreme self-confidence of Gurbachan and all drivers like him; for, with a horn like his, one felt the power and glory that belongs to the kings of the roads. For the rest of the journey, Gurbachan drove and I blew the horn.

The fellow passenger, no doubt realizing that he was locked in a taxi with two lunatics, was too terrified to say a word.

An Early Worm Finds His Books

In the year following my father's death, when my mother and stepfather left me pretty much to my own devices, books were my chief solace, my only companions. But books were hard to come by in those days.

My stepfather was not unkind to me. He seemed, rather, to be totally unaware of my existence; for, he was still in his thirties and having the good life—late-night parties, shikar trips into the forests around Dehra, frequent business trips to Delhi accompanied by my mother—adult affairs which had little interest for a ten-year-old boy home for his winter holidays.

Anyone who has read the shikar stories of that period may be forgiven for believing that those hunting expeditions were full of drama and excitement. A skilful writer like Corbett could turn the humdrum into high adventure; and he did at least go into the forest on foot. But let me assure you that there was nothing more boring than accompanying a hunting party that goes crashing through the jungle on the back of an elephant or driving down to a forest in a jeep, banging away at some unfortunate chital or sambar that happened to get in the way. It wasn't sport, it was slaughter, and most of the shikaris were of this type.

My stepfather and his buddies did most of their shooting from a jeep, usually at night with the help of strong floodlights. He was a Punjabi gentleman in the car business, and at the time he was onto a good thing, buying up surplus World War II jeeps. And it was the coming of the jeep that really led to the decimation of our wildlife. Jeeps could travel the narrow, bumpy forest roads which had been too rough for other vehicles. Now, in the last year of the war, and for some time afterwards, there were more jeeps than cars on the roads, and our so-called shikaris (who were little better than poachers, flouting every regulation in the book) found these jeeps just right for their forays into the forests.

My stepfather's friends included a sporting raja who occasionally accompanied him on these jaunts. At night they would fix some unfortunate beast in the spotlight from their jeep and then—bang, bang, bang!—there'd be roast venison and cured chital for everyone for the next few days.

And if you wanted a leopard-skin coat for memsahib, or a tiger-skin rug for the sitting room of the maharani of Titlipur, you organized a beat, in which some hundred or more villagers were engaged to move noisily through the jungle, shouting and beating empty kerosene tins until the distracted tiger was driven into the open where our brave hunters would gun it down. Believe me, there was nothing noble or courageous about the business of big game hunting, in spite of the romantic tales churned out by the more literate of these shikaris. Perched on a machan (a sturdy platform high in a tree), with a powerful rifle or shotgun in your hands, you had all the advantages. The tiger never had a chance—unless, of course, you were a very bad shot, like the aforesaid raja, who shot one of his guests by mistake. Of course, there were those wicked gossips who insisted that it was deliberate: the raja had a fancy for the friend's wife and thought this was the quickest way of winning her, but even if this was so, he was doomed to disappointment because, (as I learnt later, from our cook) she took off with the raja's aide-de-camp instead.

When my mother and father went off on these two or three-day shikar trips, I was usually left at home; but on one or two occasions they took me along, hoping perhaps to instil in me a love for big game hunting.

I have described one of these jaunts before in a story, 'Copperfield in the Jungle'. So, I will just summarize it by saying that my boredom and ennui were relieved by the discovery of a bookshelf in the forest rest house where we were staying. And, while the great hunters were dashing off into the jungle with their guns (and frequently coming back empty-handed), I discovered several authors who were to give me considerable pleasure then and in the years to come: M. R. James (*Ghost Stories of an Antiquary*), P. G. Wodehouse (*Love Among the Chickens* was my introduction to PGW), and A. A. Milne (with *The Great House Mystery*). I was always to prefer Milne's adult stories and plays to his children's stories. (I think he did, too, in the end.) Toy animals voicing human sentiments never did appeal to me. Appealing though animals may be as pets or in the wild, their civilization is different to ours. A better one, possibly; but distinct from ours. The only time I found an animal take interest in a book was when a monkey got into my Mussoorie home and tore several of my manuscripts to shreds. Some might say that he was only doing what I should have done myself, but even my worst critics haven't gone that far. I like animals, but I refuse to be sentimental about them.

Back in the 1940s, even though the visual media was restricted to the cinema, books were scarce commodities in small-town India. Anyone who was hooked on reading had to go in search of books.

Poking around in the back veranda of Granny's house on Dehra's Old Survey Road, I found a number of books, obviously untouched for years, tucked away in a chest of drawers. I had never seen my grandmother read anything apart from letters, so they could not have been hers. The name 'E. Sims' was inscribed in some of them, and I learnt later that she was a great-aunt who had died some years previously.

A few of the books were religious tracts, obviously unsuitable for an enquiring mind, but several Victorian novelists were included in the small collection, and there were two or three novels by Dickens. I picked up *Nicholas Nickleby* and carried it back to my stepfather's rented house in Dalanwala.

A fortnight later, I was back in Granny's back veranda, and this time I came up with a book of stories about South Africa. *The Little Karoo* by Pauline Smith, and *The Virginian* by Owen Wister, a precursor of the modern 'Western'. Both books had 'E. Sims' on the flyleaf, and it was clear that her tastes were nothing if not eclectic.

I never could find out much about 'E. Sims', other than that she was a distant relative, but she certainly played a formative role in my development as a reader (and possibly as a writer), because I devoured almost all the books in that small collection (including diverse works such as *Little Women* and *The Invisible Man*) and to this day remain ready to read almost anything provided it has tone, style, and quality.

Never a Dull Moment

It's mid-season in Mussoorie and I am fighting my way down the Mall Road along with thousands of tourists, both holidaymakers and locals, determined to enjoy the delight of the hill station. The car could make no progress, having been rammed into by a pram. Fortunately, the pram was empty. But as we could make better progress on foot, we abandoned the car and joined the happy throng.

Pram-pushers do good business at this time of the year, as frazzled mothers soon tire of lugging their babies around on the Mall. When my royalties dry up, I shall get a pram and make a living pushing babies around. It's easier than driving a taxi.

My destination is the Savoy, where I am to lunch with Shubhadarshini, who made a TV show called *Ek Tha Rusty* many years ago. Since then, we have both grown older and wiser.

The crowd increases as I near Gandhi Chowk, or Library Bazaar as it is known to the locals. Here, the wayside vendors are busy, selling everything from balloons and candyfloss to boiled eggs and roasted peanuts. I am persuaded to buy a boiled egg. They even peel it for me, provide me with a generous amount of salt and pepper. The pepper gets up my nose, and I start sneezing so vigorously that the crowd parts, making my progress easier.

After manoeuvring past the traffic jam at Gandhi Chowk I finally reach the Savoy. Sanctuary! Its extensive grounds and gardens give me a feeling of unfettered freedom. And I am welcomed like an old friend, for this was a favourite watering place in the old days.

I am welcomed to the Writers' Bar, given a gin and tonic, then led in a procession to the dining room where I am served shepherd's pie, my favourite dish. The management refuses to let us pay for lunch. They are not sure if I'm real, or the returning spirit of one of those famous writers whose names are commemorated on the wall of the Writers' Bar. But I look substantial enough, more flesh than spirit, and the shepherd's pie finds its true home.

Two hours later, I am on the Mall again, walking a little unsteadily in the direction of home and hearth. A cycle-rickshaw is summoned. I pour myself into it, relax like an overfed sloth bear. The rickshaw barely moves, the crowd is so dense.

A large lady keeps pace with the rickshaw. She is holding a baby in her arms.

'Can you hold the baby for a little while?' she asks, and before I could refuse, she has dumped the infant into my arms. The child does its best to remove my spectacles.

'Where are you from?' I ask the mother.

'Amritsar,' she says. 'You must come to Amritsar.'

I promise to come when my royalties run out, I can make a living as a babysitter in Amritsar. After some time, she takes the baby back and disappears into a beauty parlour. Ships that pass in the night....

Finally, I arrive at the bookshop. No one is buying books today, although some kids are looking at the colouring books on the pavement and dripping ice cream all over them. It's a hot day and ice creams have priority over books.

Someone from the crowd recognizes me, walks over, and thrusts a hundred-rupee note into my hands.

'Well, thank you very much,' I say. 'That's extremely generous of you.'

'No, no!' he says. 'I want your autograph. On the note, please.'

'But is that legal?' I ask, longing to hang on to the note.

'Of course. The RBI Governor has signed it. Gandhiji's photo is on it. You have their blessings. Please sign.'

'Wouldn't you prefer an autographed book? Only sixty rupees.'

'No, I only collect notes. See, I have one autographed by John Abraham.'

Flattered to be in such company, I gave him my autograph. Then I bought a colouring book. Colouring it would be therapy of a sort. Better than reading gory American crime novels.

The owner of the bookstore refused to take any payment for the colouring book. Instead, he suggested that I author colouring books. They sold better than books that had to be read.

And finally, I stumbled home and went to bed.

Not a bad day, after all. Shepherd's pie at the Savoy. A gin and tonic. A free colouring book. My autograph in demand—and that, too, beside the RBI Governor's. And an invitation to Amritsar to be a babysitter.

Never a dull moment on an author's off-day.

The Rope Festival

As I write, one of Landour's landmarks is disappearing—the big rock, or cluster of rocks, at the bend of the road above Claremont. This very sharp bend has always been a difficult one for vehicles to negotiate, and the only way to widen the road is to remove the massive rock outcrop. After several months of hacking away, this has now been done. And oddly enough, even as the rock face disappears, I make a fascinating discovery about the site.

A couple of hours ago, I was leafing through Surgeon General Balfour's *The Cyclopaedia of India* (the third edition of 1885), a rare three-volume tome which I acquired a few years ago, and quite by chance came across the following entry:

> RASSI-KA-MELA is a fair which since some years has been put a stop to through the Commissioner of Kumaon, who represented to the raja of Garhwal the loss of life which frequently took place during the spectacle. A rope is prepared several inches in circumference, and several hundred yards in length, made of Babur grass which grows on these hills. When finished, it is tested. A few days before the fair takes place, and a locality has been fixed upon, this rope is stretched from the hill-top,

or hill-side, to another, across some frightful yawning khud, some hundred yards in width; one end of the rope being fixed much higher than the other. On this rope is placed a large wooden horse, or imitation of one, generally painted red or blue, under which or through the horse's legs, it is so tied as to keep it in an upright horizontal position, so that is may slide from the higher to the lower end of the rope. On the day the fair comes off, thousands of hill folks collect together to witness the tamasha, music, and dancing, not forgetting hill whisky. As the hour of action approaches, the horseman gets astride of his charger, and, at a given signal, away go horse and rider, acquiring increasing impetus as they proceed; the crash at the last is fearful, horse and rider being pitched with great violence to the ground. In former years, hill rajas, their ranis and retinue, used to be present. It was customary to then have a body of matchlockmen in attendance, and as the bold rider and horse slipped down the rope, a volley was fired at them, but seldom hit; but had a casualty occurred, the venturesome rider would have been handsomely paid, and the family pensioned. After the ride is over, all present contribute according to their means, so that a goodly sum is generally collected. A Rassi-ka-Mela took place at Landour, a little above Claremont, a house half-way up the hill, and where some rocks stand at the turning of the road. One end of the rope was fixed here, and then stretched across above the Butcher-khana khud to the hill opposite, several hundred yards. Away went the rider, obtaining a frightful impetus; with great

force, horse and rider were pitched against the hillside. As they reached terra firma, the rider had his thigh and arm broken, in fact barely escaped being killed.
—*Himalaya Chronicle*

Well, that was a long time ago, and there is hardly anyone around today who has heard of the Rassi-ka-Mela, let alone the fact that it took place (on more than one occasion probably) from the heights of Landour. I can well imagine the throng of people from the surrounding villages perching on the steep slopes to watch the tamasha. I hope they contributed generously towards the reward. The rajas of Garhwal were not noted for their generosity and I doubt if the promised 'pensions' ever materialized.

Now the big rock has finally made way for the road, but there's another large rock formation on the next spur, just in case anyone wants to try this early form of paragliding.

Haiku

Rhododendrons greet you
Come again
The trees are still the same

The Smile on the Face of the Tiger

The elephants are under threat. With Haridwar and Rishikesh expanding to the north, and Dehradun and its satellite towns spreading east and west, the Rajaji National Park has been restricted to a narrow corridor hemmed in by roads and human habitation. Elephants need space, water, and vegetation, and in search of these necessities they must sometimes cross roads, fields, and railway tracks, and in the process they get into trouble.

Every year, we hear of two or three sad accidents in which elephants have been run down by oncoming railway engines. They stray on to the railway tracks, which form an inviting passage through the jungle, and are unable to judge the distance between themselves and an oncoming train. The engine driver seldom has enough time to brake to a stop. A collision is inevitable, and this mighty and noble animal is always the loser, destroyed by a man-made monster of iron and steel.

So where do the elephants go? Sometimes they rampage in the sugar cane fields, or knock down a village post office, or trample some poor cultivator to death. Elephants need more accommodation, but the jungle is an apartment without any room for expansion.

Once upon a time there were many tigers in the forests of the Doon. During World War II the jeep was invented, and poachers could drive these jeeps along narrow forest tracks, often at night, train their powerful lights on unsuspecting animals, shoot them and drive safely home with their trophies. As a boy, I was often taken along on these expeditions by a shikari stepfather. The animals never had a chance.

The tigers disappeared, found sanctuary on the far side of the Ganga, Today, several hundred enjoy their freedom in the Corbett National Park. Their numbers are gradually increasing. They have reason to smile.

Can a tiger smile? A satisfied snarl is as good as a smile.

Jim Corbett, who shot all those man-eaters and wrote stories about them, always held that tigers were essentially good-natured, even good-humoured creatures, perfectly happy to leave you alone if you left them alone. The exceptions, of course, were the man-eaters. Once a tiger had discovered how easy it was to kill a man, and then to eat him, it would lose all fear of humans. A meat-eating human might become a vegetarian, but a man-eating tiger is always a man-eater.

Some years ago, when I was physically more active than I am now, I trekked to Mandali, a little forest rest house north of Chakrata. There, I was told of a man-eater who had killed and eaten a number of people, villagers and travellers, although it could just as easily have helped itself to the cattle and sheep that grazed in the area. It was eventually shot by a forest officer just as it was attacking and mauling one of his young assistants. That same assistant, recovered from his wounds, was transferred to Orissa, and it was here, a couple of years later, that the poor man fell victim to a crocodile! From the jaws of one man-eater into the jaws of another. A strange destiny.

Do crocodiles smile? Very likely.

And what of leopards? Corbett shot a man-eating leopard at Rudraprayag in Garhwal, but not until it had accounted for over a hundred victims—people living in the area, or pilgrims on their way to the holy shrines of Badrinath and Kedarnath. Later, Corbett wrote a bestseller about the entire saga—*The Man-Eating Leopard of Rudraprayag*—and today a little stone monument (put up by our Border Roads Organisation) marks the spot where the man-eater's career was brought to an end.

Jim Corbett was a legendary hunter, but it is because of his skills as a writer that his hunting exploits are still known to us. His books are still selling. When copyright to his books expired in 2015, publishers rushed to bring out new editions of his books. The pen has outlived the gun!

Not all stories make great films, and when Corbett's *Man-Eaters of Kumaon* was filmed by Hollywood (starring Tabu and one man-eater) it failed to excite cinemagoers. Getting a tiger to act must be quite a challenge.

Some years ago, a brave young film producer tried to film a story of mine called 'The Last Tiger', which had appeared in the *Illustrated Weekly of India*. Tom Alter played a shikari. A tiger was borrowed from a touring circus. But instead of facing the cameras or the actors, the tiger kept running away—back to the circus to be in time for its dinner. The film was completed but it failed to get a cinema booking. Tom could have told you more about it.

I don't suppose leopards would be any better as actors, although they are certainly showing a disposition to enter areas of human habitation, including, I am told, a suburb of Mumbai. Ever-expanding towns and cities, such as Dehradun, bring about a steady intrusion into the natural habitats of our wild creatures, resulting in a conflict between man and beast. Up in the hills, the occasional man-eater has been active, terrifying the inhabitants of scattered farms and villages.

Certainly, leopards are more visible than they used to be, prowling around the outskirts of hill stations in search of well-fed dogs. Very rarely do they attack humans, but they fancy dog meat, and will prefer a well-fed pet to an undernourished stray. Mr Solomon was taking his beagle for an early morning walk when a leopard sprang out of the bushes and vanished with the dog, leaving its owner holding the leash. Rajiv Handa, another Landour resident, drove a leopard away from his front door, where it was lying in wait for his Bhutia mastiff. A couple of these big mastiffs are a match for a leopard, but one would have a hard time escaping with its life.

Leopards can, of course, climb trees, and monkeys are terrified of them—will even fall out of a tree in panic and sacrifice itself in the process. Colonel Powell, a former neighbour of mine, used to keep a stuffed leopard in his garden to frighten away the monkeys who would otherwise raid his plum trees. Even when that stuffed leopard was practically falling apart, the monkeys would keep away.

Well, I don't have a stuffed leopard, and this morning a

fat rhesus monkey got in through my window and took off with the pastries that had been given to me by a young reader.

I must take this loss in the right spirit. If we can make inroads into their forests, surely, they have the right to enter our homes. And, in any case, pastries are bad for my figure.

To the End of Our Days

Six, or seven—that's the age at which our essential tastes, even our obsessions—begin to be stamped on us by external impressions. They are never eradicated, even when we think we have forgotten them. To my dying day, I shall have a special fondness for the cosmos flower because I remember walking through a forest of them—or what seemed like a forest—when I was five or six. White, light purple, magenta, those fresh-faced flowers nodded to me as I played on the lawns of the Jamnagar palace grounds; and today, more than seventy years later, whenever I see the cosmos in bloom, I go among them, for they are eternal even if I am not. And to this day I like the sound of a cock crowing at break of day, because this was one of the first sounds that impinged on my brain when I was a child. A cock crowing at dawn. Harbinger of light, of optimism. 'Great day! Great day!' it seems to say. And it will not be denied.

Little things stay with us, remain with us over the years. The sound of a broom, the small jharoo, sweeping the steps or veranda takes me back to that distant but vivid childhood, and the thin, dark woman who swept the bungalow's rooms and veranda. I loved watching her at work. It seemed like a game to me and sometimes I would take the jharoo from her and sweep so vigorously that the dust rose and settled on the furniture. 'Memsahib will be angry,' she'd say, and take the broom away from me. But she'd let me borrow it from time to time, when my parents weren't around! The broom-motif has remained with me, and the other day, seeing that my steps were covered with dead leaves, I picked up the small jharoo lying outside my door and began clearing away the leaves.

A local shopkeeper on his way to the bazaar saw me sweeping away and called out: 'Sir, what are you doing? That's not your job. Give the jharoo to the sweeper!' Absorbed in my childhood hobby, all I could say was, 'Yes, memsahib,' while sending up a flurry of dead leaves. He continued on his way, muttering something about the poor old writer having lost his balance at last.

Not all our early impressions are of a pleasant nature, but they linger with us just the same. Like the frequent quarrels that took place between my parents, oftentimes in my presence. I hated these quarrels, and I was quite helpless to stop them. Eventually they led to my parents' separation. And all my life I have felt profoundly disturbed if I see or overhear a husband and wife quarrelling bitterly. I look around to see if a child is present. And then realize that I am that child.

Fortunately, the most lasting impressions are the harmonious ones. Why do I still prefer homemade butter to factory-made butter? Because, when I was five or six, I would watch my father vigorously beating up a bowl of cream and then spreading a generous amount of creamy white butter on my toast. Now Beena, who looks after the household, knows why I am always demanding creamy white homemade butter for breakfast.

And you, dear reader, will have, similar impressions to carry with you all your days. That first day at school, maybe an agonizing parting from your parents. The face of a loved one lost. A pullover knitted by your granny. A favourite toy. A doll, perhaps. A book of rhymes, tattered and torn. Someone who gave you a flower, a kiss on the forehead. To the end of your days, you will carry that kiss with you. And may it protect you from all harm.

Where Have All the Flowers Gone?

New day. I awoke to grey skies, mist, a leaden atmosphere. But then the sun broke through, gilding the rooftops, slipping through the half-open window, lighting up the papers on my desk. The first miracle of the day. Now I must acknowledge the miracle and write a few lines glorifying the sun.

So where are my reading glasses? Here, right in front of me, so close that I missed them. The lenses need cleaning. Some of Delhi's smog still clings to them. Landour would not approve. And here I am, back on my hilltop, pen in hand, spectacles balanced on my nose. A new day has begun.

Give me the sun and the open skies. I salute the earthworm, but I would rather watch this purple butterfly as it settles on a cosmos, drinking deep of its nectar.

The cosmos! My favourite flower. So clean, so fresh on the open hillside. As a small boy, I would wander down a glade full of cosmos, looking up at their white and mauve and magenta heads nodding above me.

In recent years, the cosmos has disappeared from Mussoorie and Landour hillsides. Climate change, perhaps. Or too much building. No space left for space-loving flowers. I had to go all the way to Cloud End (some 11 kilometres from Landour) to find a new cosmos. Along with some deeply bronzed marigolds, they were enjoying the late autumn sunshine.

When I was young, I used to walk a lot. In my eighties, I find it difficult to scramble up and down slippery hill slopes. But from my window I can still see the little pine knoll, on a spur below Pari Tibba, which I would visit during those early years in Mussoorie. I called it my place of power.

The Worth of Writers

Time passes, having nothing else to do. But we change, our surroundings change, our country changes. And so, I am often asked: 'You have lived in India for most of your life—almost eighty years—what are the most remarkable changes you have seen?'

Well, change comes slowly, not with a great rush; and although there are certain dramatic events that stand out across the years—Independence, Partition, conflicts with our neighbours, assassinations, communal strife, scientific progress, technological advancement—the actual pace and tenor of everyday life is much as it used to be. Those wedding tents and feasts are still the fulcrum of social life. We follow cricket in preference to other sports purely out of habit; only we do it via the television rather than those dear old transistor radios with their running commentaries. The 'Binaca Hit Parade' is long gone but Bollywood still supplies the hit songs of the day.

The middle class has grown and prospered, and as a result people are better dressed today. The fashion industry barely existed back in the 1950s and 60s. You were 'with it' if you could get into a pair of jeans. I could never find a pair of jeans that would comply with my figure, so I have remained in baggy pants from the Chaplin–Raj Kapoor era to the present day.

Only yesterday a kind soul from Kerala gave me a lungi, saying it would improve my appearance. It does indeed but as an icy wind from Tibet is at this moment ripping around my ankles, I shall postpone the wearing of the lungi to summer.

I have never been able to keep up with the fashion in haircuts, still clinging to the short back and sides of my schooldays. The youngsters in my home at present all look like porcupines, with their hair standing on end like wire brushes. I believe this is done with the help of some kind of gel which can also be used for sealing envelopes and parcels. I must give it a try. I mean the gel, not the hairstyle.

People, people everywhere. This is one change that you can't help noticing if you have been around for some time. The number of human beings on planet earth, and in our part of the world, in particular, has gone up by leaps and bounds. I can't say this is a bad thing. The loving union of man and woman usually results in human offspring, and, as Tagore said, 'Every child comes with the message that God is not yet tired of man.'

But the earth grows tired. For hundreds of thousands of years, it has been sustaining millions, now billions of humans who, more than bird, beast, reptile, or insect, have been helping themselves to the earth's resources without putting anything back. How much longer can this good earth sustain the human race? Already there is talk of mass migration to other planets. All I can say is, the sooner the better!

For one who loves this earth, this land, the prospect is a little depressing, even though I won't be around to see it.

What I do see today, in almost every town or city I visit, are mountains of garbage, growing higher by the day, stagnating in the sun and rain, so foul that even the crows and stray dogs stay away. A certain amount of rubbish has always been turned out into the streets, but not with the devil-may-care speed that is apparent today.

> From plastic bags to polythene
> The prospect is far from clean

Oh, for the good old days of paper bags. Those paper bags are made from discarded exercise books, exam papers, and unwanted film and fashion magazines. How quickly they would deteriorate, 'dissolve and resolve themselves into a dew' as Hamlet said about his too, too solid flesh.

As a writer, I have mixed feelings about paper bags. How well I remember the day when the lad who looked after his father's ration shop down the road came to me and said, 'Uncle, you have so many books, can you give me one?' Always happy to encourage a youngster to read, I presented him my latest—a large-format children's book handsomely produced by the National Book Trust. A day later, walking by his shop, I stopped to buy some gur, for which I have a weakness. And, lo and behold, the gur was presented to me in a handsome paper bag made out of the pages of my own book!

My author's ego was shattered. All those words, so carefully inscribed on paper, were worth no more than a piece of gur.

Only the other day on a television show, one of our leaders declared that writers in India were of no consequence, and I can't help feeling he was right.

Still, if paper bags could replace plastic bags, I would gladly sacrifice the pages on which I have written this piece. But only after it has appeared in the *Sunday Times*.

I must be one of the few writers still standing or rather sitting, who writes by hand, that is, with a ballpoint pen. This is not because I am stubborn and out-of-date but simply because I express myself better when I am in close contact with pen and paper. There are two old, discarded typewriters in my house, in case anyone wants one. There are also two laptops, jealously guarded by my grandchildren, who are up all night on Facebook, keeping up with their friends in the 'virtual' world, whatever that may be.

I like to sleep at night, and I love gazing at the stars—especially up here in the mountains, where the skies are usually so clear—and I remember romantic moments, when the moon and the stars combined to make those moments more magical. But being a pragmatic fellow, I also believe in a good night's sleep. For the morrow I must face the 'real' world—electricity bills (but no light), school bills, publishers' deadlines, blocked drainpipes, leaking roofs etc., many of the things that you, dear reader, have to cope with too. Never mind:

> When all the wars are done,
> And all the garbage gone,
> A butterfly will still be beautiful, my son.

Why Smart Cities?

It's good to know that my old friend the jackfruit is finally coming into its own. Apparently, it is now much in demand in western countries, a fashionable substitute for meat fillings for burgers, sandwiches, pies etc., with one enthusiast even calling it 'mutton hanging from a tree'.

Here in India, we have always appreciated a good jackfruit curry, or even better, a jackfruit pickle. I'm a pickle fiend myself, and among the twenty different pickles on my sideboard there is always a jar of jackfruit pickle; that's why I call it an old friend. But I had no idea it tasted like mutton. The seed and the pulp have their own individual flavour. As it grows on a tree, we call it fruit, but we cook it as though it were a vegetable. And if, to some, it tastes like mutton, then perhaps some meat eaters will become vegetarians. On the other hand, some vegetarians might not care for its meaty flavour!

When I was a boy, we had an old jackfruit tree growing beside the side veranda. I spent a lot of time in the trees surrounding my grandmother's bungalow, and this one was easy to climb. The others included several guava and litchi trees, lemons and grapefruits, and, of course, a couple of mango trees—but these last were difficult to climb.

'Why do you spend so much time in the trees?' complained my grandmother. 'Why not do something useful for a change?'

'The trees are my brothers,' I would say, 'I like to play with them.'

And I still think of them as my brothers, although I can no longer climb trees or play in them.

And, indeed, I think of them as human beings possessed of individuality and charm. Just as no two humans are exactly alike (unless they happen to be twins), so no two trees are the same. Like humans they grow from seed. They develop branches as arms and leaves like flowing hair. We give birth to children; they give birth to fruits and flowers. We shelter our young, they shelter small creatures of the forest.

But, unlike us, they spring from the soil, from the land— that very land that gives us food and pasture and protection; the land that we so casually take for granted, preferring to build upon it rather than grow upon it. Where will our cattle graze when the last green spaces have gone?

'No problem', says a young friend. 'We can always import our milk.'

The other day I came across an old book that had been on my shelves for many years: *Farmer's Glory* by A. G. Street, written over sixty years ago. In his epilogue he writes:

> It is perhaps nothing to boast about, but there is little doubt that the present prosperity of British farming is mainly due to one man, who is now dead. His name was

Adolf Hitler. There is no disputing that it was the fear of famine during the early 1940s that taught the British nation that despite all man's cleverness and inventions, when real danger comes an island people must turn for succour to the only permanent asset they possess, the land of their own country. It has never, and will never, let them down; always provided they realise and obey this eternal truth—that to make the land serve man, man must first be content to serve the land.

And surely it is this love of the land and willingness to serve it that is at the heart of patriotism. The patriotic songs and speeches that we hear from time to time are fine for stirring up the emotions, but it is really the connect between ourselves and the 'do bigha zamin' on which we grow our fruit and grain that emboldens us to protect it.

I think I am correct in saying that most of our jawans, the young men who join the solid ranks of the Indian Army, come from rural backgrounds; some from the hills, some from the vast plains and hinterland of our country. They know the value of the land. They have grown up in the villages and have worked with their families in the rice fields, or sugar cane plantations, or mango groves, or wheat or corn or mustard or other fields of an infinite variety of crops. More than the city folk, they know the value of the land, its true worth in terms of either prosperity or poverty. And so, they are ready to defend it, to fight for it against all comers. The best soldiers come from the soil that they and their forefathers have tilled. So, let us protect the land—not only from the intruder or the enemy, but from those who would turn the field or the forest into one more concrete jungle.

But, of course, there are those who prefer concrete jungles. Like my young friend who wants to live in a smart city and never mind the cities that are no longer smart. My advice to him (unheeded, of course) is to go back to his roots, create a smart little village, and plant jackfruit trees!

The Power of Pen and Paper

While it is true that I do most of my writing by hand, this does not mean that I will use any pencil or pen that comes to hand. Kind people often give me fountain pens as gifts, unaware that for me the fountain pen is a formidable form of technology, designed with the express purpose of tormenting me. Being one of the clumsiest humans on earth, I am unable to fill or refill or empty a fountain pen of its ink without getting the said ink, black, blue or blue-black, all over my hands or onto my coat sleeves or shirt front. I will then ruin a good handkerchief trying to wipe myself clean. On one account, unable to locate a handkerchief, I reached for the nearest piece of cloth, only to realize (too late) that it was a lady's dupatta. That's one way of how to lose friends and fail to influence people.

No, the good old ballpoint is the pen for me. It doesn't make a mess and it can be thrown away when its usefulness is over. There is no bottle of ink waiting to be typed over on to my writing pad.

Back in my early schooldays, we were equipped with penholders into which nibs had to be inserted. Each student was also given a small inkwell which fitted into a hole in his desk. You had to dip your pen into this little pot of black ink, and then scratch away for a line or two before making another foray into the inkwell. This was a laborious process and often a messy one; but this was how Dickens and Kipling and Tagore and Premchand wrote their novels—dip and scratch, dip and scratch, for days and weeks and months on end. It also meant that you had to take some care of your handwriting, so that the compositor (in the case of an author) or a teacher (in the case of a student) could make out what had been written.

My father used to say that you could judge a man by his handwriting. Mahatma Gandhi had a good, clear hand; so did Abraham Lincoln. Hitler's handwriting deteriorated as time went by, denoting a similar deterioration in his thought process. But a neat handwriting did not necessarily mean you were a good person. Thomas Griffiths Wainewright, the notorious serial poisoner, had an elegant handwriting; but then, he was also a neat poisoner.

My father wrote a clear, fluent, open script, and he always enjoined on me the importance of good handwriting. Use large letters, he always told me; write with a bold hand; don't skimp on paper; don't try to squeeze a lot of words into a small space. An open handwriting denotes an open and uncluttered mind. And I think he was right.

Over the years, over these many, many years, I have done most of my writing by hand, only occasionally resorting to a typewriter. As a boy, I went to the trouble of taking shorthand and typing lessons; but soon shorthand became obsolete, and now typewriters are obsolete. My great-grandson's laptop looks as though it may also be obsolete very shortly. Fortunately, my writing hand is in good shape, and I can still put down a thousand words before breakfast without any difficulty. If my hand is still in good shape it is probably because it has been wielding a pen or pencil all these years.

When asked how one became a writer, William Saroyan said: 'Paper and pencil will do.' It was, of course, a simplification, but there is something about putting pen to paper that is physically as well as mentally satisfying. There is a certain sensuous intimacy about this connection, an intimacy that is absent from any other form of writing. Maybe it's the texture and touch of the paper, the flow of ink, the movement of the pen, the connection of all three with the human hand and the hand's connection with the mind of the writer. It all amounts to the power of the pen, not forgetting the paper.

Mark Twain tried an experiment to see if he could convey his thoughts to someone simply by putting them down on paper—and leaving them there.

He wrote a long letter to a friend but instead of posting it he crumpled it up and dropped it in his wastepaper basket. A week later, he met his friend who told him that he had been constantly thinking of the writer and that he had been aware of Mark Twain's own thoughts and feelings, almost as though they had been communicated through some intangible means.

Mark Twain then wrote a letter to one of his publishers, complaining of a delay in royalty payments. He did not post the letter. But a few days later he received his royalties!

Fellow writers who have issue with their publishers can try this method of obtaining satisfaction. However, I give no guarantee that it will work.

Discovering the Joy of Selfies

A little solitude now and then is good for the soul and good for the pen. And it is not only writers who need it. We could all do with a few hours of solitary confinement—not in a jail cell but in a room or quiet corner of our own choice. How else can we get to know ourselves?

Not everyone is in a position to renounce the material world and live in a humble dwelling on the banks of the Ganga above Rishikesh to meditate and ponder the meaning or absence of meaning in our transitory existence in a world that has been mismanaged by its human tenants.

Children have to be fed, marriages brokered, and cars topped up with petrol. The great saints and sages looked to the mountains for solitude. The great poets and prose writers—Tagore, Wordsworth, Stevenson, Melville, Conrad—turned to the rivers, lakes, seas, and oceans. The mountains are static, but water is always on the move, there is no stopping it.

Probably the best work on solitude was Defoe's *Robinson Crusoe*. Here was an intelligent man who, shipwrecked upon an uninhabited island, had solitude forced upon him. Most men would have gone mad after a year or two of complete isolation. But Crusoe learnt to adapt to the conditions and even appreciate his enforced solitude. The arrival of man Friday proved at first to be unsettling, but their chemistry proved to be just right, and loneliness became companionship.

Solitude is a condition appreciated only by a small minority. It seems to me that most people are scared of being left on their own, for almost every human activity is carried out on a crowded scale.

As a boy, inspired by Thoreau's *Walden*, I sought out a Walden Pond for myself, and discovered a wilderness outside Dehradun where a hot spring emerged from a dry riverbed. I would go there often on my bicycle. There were no other visitors, just occasionally a village boy grazing his cows.

Last year, I visited the same spot, although no longer on a bicycle. Hotels, restaurants, a veritable bazaar had come up on the banks of a tiny stream, but of the original hot spring there was no sign. In shock, it had probably gone underground.

In order to protect yourself from solitude or finding yourself on your own you can now equip yourself with a phone that takes 'selfies' and take pictures of yourself with waterfalls and cheering crowds in the background; but take care you don't step backwards into the waterfall.

Strangely along the road below my mountain home I encountered a smart young person who wanted to take a picture of both of us with her 'selfie stick'. I could hardly object. So we sat on the parapet, cheek to cheek, while she attempted to get us both in the frame of her phone camera. All she got was her pretty left ear and my red nose, but I didn't mind, it was a long time since I'd sat cheek to cheek with a pretty young thing on a parapet wall. There's something to be said for 'selfies'.

And so, I take issue with a gentleman on a TV programme who maintained that 'selfies' were a form of narcissism, denoting some form of psychological deficiency in the owner's make-up. To me, they appear to be quite harmless, fun things, provided you don't fall off a cliff or a high-rise building.

The mirror—especially that dressing table mirror—is probably the most addictive form of narcissism, and it has been around for centuries. 'Get away from that mirror!' my aunt would scream at me whenever I lingered in front of it for several minutes, trying my best to train my hair into a puff similar to the one sported by Dev Anand or Alan Ladd or whoever was the big male star that year. Nowadays, you don't see stars with puffs, possibly because they go bald rather early. Must be all this pollution.

But to return to solitude, the only place where I can find it is in my own small room looking out over the mountains. But even here I must keep my windows closed if I am not to be joined by the monkeys.

There's one particular monkey that has been looking at me speculatively through the window glass all morning. Being short-sighted I can't tell if it's a male or a female, but it makes no difference, they all have a strange desire to make off with my pyjamas. Is it because I like brightly coloured pyjamas? Or is it some sort of Freudian simian obsession which can only be explained by that psychologist on the TV channel?

Anyway, my pyjamas disappear at the rate of one a month. I have only to leave the window open for half a minute, and away goes my pyjamas, over the trees and far away.

There must be a part of the forest where a whole tribe of rhesus monkeys is prancing around in my many-coloured pyjamas. They are probably having their own fashion show.

Why I Miss the Good Old GP

Customs change with the changing times, but not always for the better.

I do miss the old GP, the family doctor, who would turn up at your house at short notice. You had only to give him a ring or send him a message saying you or one of your loved ones was down with the flu or mumps or some mysterious fever, and he'd be around in a jiffy. Years of experience enabled him to make a quick and usually accurate diagnosis and he'd write out a prescription on the spot. If he thought it was something very serious, he'd direct you to the nearest hospital. If he was a good doctor, his very presence would make you feel better. He'd put his stethoscope to your chest, feel your pulse, look at your tongue, prod your tummy, and make you breathe deeply, and say 'Aaah!' You took his pills religiously, and sooner or later you felt better.

Such doctors are a dying breed. Today, young doctors open smart clinics or join city hospitals, and if you want to see them you must stand in line with dozens of other patients. In spite of all the advances of medical science, sick people multiply by the day and our cities are flooded with nursing homes and diagnostic centres. Strange that in this age of scientific and medical wonders, the world should be sicker than ever.

Diabetes, impotency, heart disease, cancer, and various viral infections ensure that our medical services are overstretched. Gone are the days when a worried parent would say: 'Send for the doctor'. Now it's 'Go to the doctor' or 'Send for an ambulance'. No one is likely to come and sit by your bedside.

So, I miss those doctors, now retired or long gone, who would do just that. There was Dr Jwala Prasad, for instance, a dear man who smoked quite heavily, and who owned one of the three or four cars that plied on the Mussoorie roads back in the 1960s and 70s. He was famous for his phrase 'Nothing to worry about'. No matter how ill you were, in pain, or racked with a fever, he'd pat you on the shoulder and say, 'Nothing to worry about. You're going to be fine!'

And it actually helped! Such is the psychology of illness or wellness.

Another friendly neighbourhood doctor who I miss is Dr Bisht. I had only to ring him up, to tell him I was in dire straits, and ten minutes later I would hear the splutter of his old scooter as it drew up below my steps. 'Pulse is a bit fast today,' he'd say, after a brief examination. 'It's the blood pressure again. Don't tell me you have fallen in love again?'

'What's that got to do with it, doctor?'

'Falling in love always raises the blood pressure.'

In his infinite wisdom he'd hit the nail on the head—or the lover on his aching heart. The remedy? A long walk in the woods. 'Keep walking. That will do the trick.' His theory was that a little exercise was the best remedy for most ailments.

Well, the good doctor has long since retired, but the other day I met him when he was enjoying an outing with his grandchildren, and I could see that he was most anxious to do something for my well-being. At eighty, I do still occasionally fall in love, but on this occasion, I had nothing to complain of—no dizziness, no irregular heartbeat, no melancholia or other symptoms of the lovesick—just a seasonal cold. So, I told him I had a cold.

'Take plenty of vitamin C,' he advised. 'And drink lots of water.' Well, I have been taking vitamin C for a week, and I am looking like a lemon, and passed a lot of water, but a cold is a cold and it will go in its own good time.

I haven't been so lucky with dentists. As a small boy I had protruding teeth, so my mother took me to Dr Kapadia in Dehradun, a famous dentist in his time. But a painful prod from one of his instruments resulted in my screaming and kicking him on the shin. 'Take this boy away,' he told my mother. 'Don't bring him here again.' With the result that I still have protruding front teeth.

But it's better than having dentures. I have an elderly actor friend who was given the role of Count Dracula in one of those vampire films which are all the fashion these days. The trouble is, he wears dentures, false teeth, and when he grins or grimaces, he doesn't look at all like a vampire.

'You'll never get those teeth into a beautiful neck,' I told him. 'We'll have to do something about them.'

So, I took him to one of those street dentists who ply their trade on the outskirts of our pilgrim towns. He took out his file and sharpened my friend's false incisors until they glittered. Our hero looked like a real vampire with the sharpened incisors. But he didn't get the part. On taking the heroine into his arms and attempting to plunge his teeth into her beautiful neck, his dentures shot out and he was left toothless.

As Donald Trump would say: Sad.

Making Your Own Bed

Whenever a young person asks me for some really serious advice, I say: 'Always make your own bed.' And my young friend goes away laughing, saying: 'Bond uncle is never serious about anything.' But I am dead serious. Making one's own bed is a stamp of personality, a statement about being someone different upon this earth, a unique expression of one's individuality. Don't leave it to your mother or sister or the domestic help; it will become their kind of bed, and you will have to fit your personality to suit theirs.

Apart from that, it can be a matter of self-preservation. Not so long ago I was put up in a guest house on the edge of the desert near Jodhpur in Rajasthan. At night I retired to my room. The bed was neatly made. Too neat for my liking. I lifted the pillow and discovered a large black scorpion welcoming me with sting upraised. Well, I am not one to kill any one of God's creatures without good reason, and so, using a pencil (they have their uses), I tipped the scorpion into a large plastic mug, opened a window, and deposited the visitor into a flower bed.

Returning to the bed, I decided upon a little rearrangement of the mattresses, and on lifting one up, discovered an entire nest of scorpions. Disturbed by the interference, scores of young scorpions were soon scampering about the bed sheets. I made a tactical retreat. The railway station was not far away, and I spent the night on an armchair in the station waiting room. Better a railway bug than a desert scorpion! Making my own bed was something I learnt in my school days when, as a boarder, you were at the mercy of prefects, housemasters, and occasional pranksters. You made your own bed, polished your own shoes, and washed behind the ears with Lifebuoy soap. Occasionally, a bright spark would introduce some stinging nettle between your sheets, and you would retaliate in kind, preferably with a spiky cactus. 'French' beds were popular. You rearranged the sheets in such a way that the occupant, getting between them, found himself in an inextricable tangle.

All this meant that you had to be very protective of your bed. Not only did you make your own bed, but you had to guard against all kinds of interlopers.

I became so protective of my bed that when I went to London as a young man and rented a bed-sitting room from a motherly Jewish landlady, I had a regular tussle with her over who had the right to make my bed. She insisted that I was her boarder, with a right to sharing the bathroom; she had a right to tidying my bedroom, including the bed. I would make the bed. She would remake it. I would make it again. Sometimes she won; sometimes I won. In the end we compromised. She would make the bed in the morning so I wouldn't be late for work. And in the evenings, when I returned, I could make it again! When winter came, this kind lady produced an old-fashioned stone hot-water bottle, which was most effective. It kept my feet warm all night. As a result, I surrendered all bed-making rights to my landlady.

A warm bed and a good breakfast, what more can a young man ask for?

Good breakfasts can be had in many of our starred hotels, but I have never really been happy with the beds. For a start, there are far too many pillows. These are flung away before I lie down. How can one sleep propped up like the desiccated corpse in *Psycho*?

Then the sheet and blankets have to be loosened, as these are always wedged into the mattress too tightly. Then the mattresses are often too springy and propel you towards the ceiling if you flop on to them suddenly. I have sometimes found it easier to sleep on the floor, using a pillow and blanket from the bed and a thick rug beneath me.

Hotel rooms are very similar to each other, so don't forget your room number. On one occasion I stepped out of my room, leaving the door slightly ajar, to see if there was a stairway at the end of the corridor. (I'm paranoid about lifts and avoid them if I can). On returning to the room, the door being open, I found the bed occupied by a large lady in a pink nightdress. I was in the wrong room! Fortunately, the lady did not scream, and I backed out, apologizing profusely. She seemed to recognize me, even though she got my name wrong.

'Aren't you that writer fellow, Bumskin Rond?' she asked in good humour. 'Come on in and have a martini.'

Fond as I am of martinis, I thought it wise to beat a hasty retreat.

Stick to your own bedroom, Bumskin.

Boy from the Jungle

Rudyard Kipling made his name with his 'barrack-room' verse and short stories, first published in Indian newspapers. He then wrote two novels: *The Light That Failed*, which failed; and *Kim*, which was a glorious success. But it was with *The Jungle Book*, and its successor, *The Second Jungle Book*, that Kipling really entered the land of the immortals. Mowgli, jungle boy, wolf-boy, friend and companion of wild creatures with whom he grew up, is now a part of almost every young reader's literary experience. Mowgli combines innocence with a natural intelligence. His familiarity with jungle love, his camaraderie, and his inborn human rationality help him to survive the rigours of jungle life and to get the better of his sworn enemy, Shere Khan the tiger. Kipling did not spend much time in the Indian jungles. He was essentially a city man—Lahore, Allahabad, Simla, and the big railway junctions.

Most of his jungle love came from his father, Lockwood Kipling, who had spent most of his life in India, and whose book, *Beast and Man in India*, provided Rudyard with themes and background material for his jungle stories.

This was especially the case with the story 'Toomai of the Elephants' which together with 'Rikki-Tikki-Tavi' is one of the most appealing and popular of Kipling's stories for children; for we must remember that not all of *The Jungle Book* is Mowgli; there are, in fact, only three Mowgli stories in the first *Jungle Book*; the remaining four belong to *The Second Jungle Book*. 'Toomai' was so popular that in 1937 the great documentary film-maker Robert Flaherty came to India to film the story. He found a real elephant-boy to play the part of Toomai. This was Sabu, a simple but gifted youth from the jungles of Mysore. The resultant film, *Elephant Boy*, was such a success that Sabu was taken to England, where he acted as Mowgli in *The Jungle Book* (1942). Hollywood beckoned, and Sabu achieved stardom without ever losing his charm and grace; but he died young, unable to cope with the fast life and materialism of this glamorous new world. We do not know if Kipling's Mowgli made a success of his return to civilization. Real wolf-boys seldom did. There were instances, in Kipling's time, and after, when children were found roaming in the forests, apparently brought up by wild beasts. But these were usually poor, undernourished creatures, moving around on all fours, unable to speak or communicate with humans. Rescued from the wild, they did not survive for long. So, Kipling's notion of a wolf-boy was a very romantic one.

He wrote *The Jungle Book* and *Kim* when he was living in 'exile' in America, unhappy there, and missing the India where he had lived and worked for seven years. Not only was he a misfit in America, but it was there that he lost his daughter, the little girl for whom he had written the *Just So Stories*. Only one book came out of his American experience, the short novel *Captains Courageous*; but it was during these unhappy four or five years that he did most of his best work, and almost all of it looking back upon his time in India: *Kim,* the *Jungle Books, Just So Stories,* the stories in *Many Inventions....* By the time *Kim* was published (1904), he received the Nobel Prize for Literature. He was to write many more stories, verse and travelogues, but somehow, he could never recapture the magic that went into the two *Jungle Books* and *Kim.* One can write of a great love only when one has been parted from it. In his later years, Kipling was reviled as an imperialist and a reactionary. Singing the praises of the empire, he sang out of season, and he paid for it. By the time he died in 1936, he was out of favour, and out of fashion, even in his own land. But as one columnist in a New York paper wrote: 'What difference does it make if he is an insufferable Tory? He wrote *The Jungle Book.* Has everybody forgotten that?' And today, that is what everybody remembers. Not Kipling, the super patriot, but Kipling, the creator of Mowgli, Bagheera, Kaa, Rikki-Tikki-Tavi, Kala Nag, and Little Toomai.... Little Toomai, who had seen what no man had seen before—the dance of the elephants at night, alone in the heart of the jungle!

IT'S A WONDERFUL LIFE

*Lockdown Journals
(April–May 2020)*

'If I am not for myself, who will be for me?
And if I am not for others, what am I?
And if not now, when?'

—Hillel the Elder

1 April 2020

It's time to do some writing.

'Something to cheer people up,' said David Davidar on the phone the other day.

Ho-hum. First, I have to cheer myself up. Over the years—and that stretched back many decades—I have tried religiously to procure five hundred words of wit, wisdom, or nonsense every morning, in order to prove that I am a writer worthy of his salt, or at least of breakfast. I believe P. G. Wodehouse did a thousand words every day, and Hemingway did even more, in spite of a hangover. I am not in the same class, and I do not suffer from hangovers, in spite of the occasional rum punch before dinner. But I do suffer from bouts of inertia, especially after breakfast. It must be the pickle.

Anyway, just as I am about to put pen to paper and satisfy my eager readers (two? three?) with an ode to the crow on my windowsill, I am overcome by a sudden urge to sleep. You could call it my mid-morning siesta (in Mexico, they have two siestas: the second one in order to recover from the first). The pen falls from my hand. Plonk. My head falls on my writing pad. Bonk. The startled crow departs. And I am asleep at my desk for roughly half an hour.

Beena, or Rakesh, brings me to life with a mug of coffee.

They also bring me up to date with the latest coronavirus statistics. I won't repeat them here, you know them better than I do, for you have only to switch on the TV set to be presented with all the depressing details of the pandemic.

'Trump says it will all be over in two weeks,' says Rakesh.

'He said it two weeks ago, and we're still in the thick of it.'

'He should consult Pandit—,' Beena names her favourite astrologer.

'He probably did,' I say, not being a fan of astrologers. 'This virus determines its own course, without consulting the stars.'

We left it at that, and I finally got on with my five hundred words.

The case of the coughing tiger. It sounds like a Perry Mason mystery, but it's fact not fiction.

The otherwise healthy tiger in the Bronx Zoo in New York city has been diagnosed with the coronavirus. Apparently, she got it from her keeper. She hasn't passed it on to anyone, but now everyone is looking suspiciously at their pets, especially cats.

Cats were once the companions of witches, and I hope there won't be a cat-hunt similar to the witch-hunt of old. I happen to like cats. Many years ago, I kept a Siamese cat called Suzie, but it eloped with a Manx cat (these don't have tails), and I felt rebuffed and kept a dog instead.

But cats are different from other animals. I'm convinced they are psychic. They see things that we don't. They are in league with the supernatural.

In her old age, my grandmother kept a Persian cat. She was very attached to granny, and when the old lady died, the bereaved cat became very moody, wouldn't eat for days, and roamed about the house and garden in search of her late mistress. Then one day, her mood changed, and she became quite cheerful and friendly again.

One afternoon, I heard her purring contentedly in what had been granny's bedroom. And putting my head around the door, I saw the cat reclining at the foot of the bed, her ears laid back, tail waving, and eyes focused. For a second or two, I saw granny standing there, stroking the cat, smiling down at her. Then the vision was gone. Perhaps it was my imagination. But I was often to find the cat reclining on a sofa or garden bench, purring softly, while an invisible hand stroked her gently.

5 April 2020

In a broken and contentious world, it can be difficult for an individual to find the happiness that he seeks, even if by nature he (or she) is not a contentious person. It is difficult to enjoy the flowers by the wayside if a tear gas cylinder (or something worse) has just burst in front of you. Throughout history the peace-loving, happiness-seeking individual is caught in the crossfire of human conflict. But still, he grows flowers, and sometimes he gets to enjoy them.

If you can grow flowers in your garden, or on your balcony, or on your windowsill, you have a chance of finding happiness—fleeting moments of it, anyway.

From my bedroom window I can see a storm brewing over the distant hills. The sky has darkened. The wind is a low moan as it channels a pathway through the trees. Lightning strikes at random, zigzagging across the evening sky. Nature at her most elemental but also most beautiful.

That lightning, the violence of the storm, are not aimed at me or mine, for the elements take no sides. I can stand and watch the beauty of this electrical display, knowing it is indifferent to the watcher. Lightning will strike by accident, not design.

I close the window and turn on the television. Tired,

desperate refugees from bombed-out homes in Syria trek across no-man's land in search of something and are turned back from another border. They sleep out in the open, the children shivering, hungry.

In America, a lone gunman goes on the rampage; a 'disturbed' individual. But we are all disturbed individuals. Trump shakes his head, talks about money; there are white circles around his eyes; he is losing colour!

In New Delhi, there are communal riots. This suits many of the politicians. In Indonesia, an earthquake, nature asserting herself. We are obsessed with outer space, forgetting the fires smouldering within our planet, ready to erupt without prior notice. This, the only green planet as far as we know, is looking less green by the day. There will be many Pompeiis.

7 April 2020

Grow something, my friend. Even if it is a potted tomato plant, it will make a difference to your life.

A bowl of tomatoes is on the table before me. It's two o'clock, and the afternoon sun slants through the west window, falling on the tomatoes and giving them a certain resplendence. They glow. They glow like—well, like tomatoes in the sun.

At one time, these blood-red 'love apples' were considered poisonous, until a brave man came along and consumed a basket of them in public. Now we add tomatoes to all our dishes. Eating would be a dull business without a tomato to flavour the curry or the roast or the soup.

But this essay is not about eating. I have gone through life eating what is put in front of me, without fuss or favour. My grandmother saw to that. Eat your porridge, or go hungry. This was emphasized when I was at boarding school. Rhubarb as a sweet dish, every day all summer. This was because our headmaster grew rhubarb in his back garden, and decided to inflict it on us. He probably charged extra for it, too. (Cynicism comes early at a boarding school.) And when I was in London, dashing off to work without breakfast, I would be sustained by Marmite sandwiches. Good old Marmite!

And I have a jar on my table, sixty-five year, later.

But I was praising the tomato not so much for its nourishment, but for its shape, its texture, its colour. An artist's delight. Why paint apples when you have tomatoes?

The tomato is a sensual berry. Bite into it and the generous juices spill out over your lips, your chin, your hands—the nectar of the gods. Only the mango is more sensual. A mango will make love to you, if you allow it to do so. The apple belongs to cold countries. Rarely will its juices trickle down your chin. Only a few western writers have possessed the gift of sensuality. A. E. Coppard and H. E. Bates displayed it to some extent in their short stories, but it would be hard to find a novelist who did so. Mary Webb, perhaps, in *Gone to Earth* or André Gide in *Fruits of the Earth*, or the artist Aubrey Beardsley in a few pieces in *The Yellow Book*.

It takes an artist to appreciate the sensual—a Renoir, a Manet, a Monet, a Gauguin.... Gauguin in Tahiti! What a combination! A great artist's sensual nature comes to fruition in a decaying paradise.

What am I doing, writing about tomatoes and the sensual nature of plants when hundreds of thousands around the world are perishing from the effects of swift-moving and cunning coronavirus? Not everyone succumbs. It is hard on a few, easy on others. It is almost as if it is playing a game of its own. 'Eeni-meeni-maini-mo, Catch a fellow by his toe!' Or rather, his throat.

Choosing its victims at random. One day a bus conductor, the next day a prime minister. (And Mr Johnson did look so vulnerable, unlike the boastful Trump.) Has artificial intelligence run amuck?

Is this nature hitting back, after all the injuries done to it by humans? Or is it a man-made virus, a chemical weapon that has cut loose, making fools of the scientists and world leaders who have brought it into being?

So here we are, locked up in our houses for days on end, hoping for a good hot summer to drive the pestilence away. Or maybe a deep freeze.

It will move in its own time, and meanwhile, we must give some meaning to our own lives and learn to live like Robinson Crusoe abandoned on his lonely island, with or without man Friday.

Well, at least he had an island at his disposal—trees, running water, coconuts, fish, and turtles' eggs for breakfast.

Respect your breakfast, said Manu the lawgiver. Actually, he said 'respect your food', which, for me, means breakfast since is the meal which sets me up for the day. And it is going to be a long day, as the world staggers through another twenty-four hours of bad news and gloomy predictions.

Mine is a simple but substantial breakfast. Three toasts. One crowned with a fried egg. The second is buttered and topped with a little garlic pickle. The third is left to my discretion. I may or may not consume it, depending upon my mood and appetite. It's like a small insurance policy.

Well, a week ago, when all this lockdown fuss began, I looked down at my first toast to find that the customary fried egg was no longer smiling up at me.

'Where's my egg?' I cried out like a lost soul.

'No eggs in town,' said Beena from the kitchen. 'But

there's a nice fried tomato on your toast. You like tomatoes, don't you?'

As I had only just written a poem in praise of the tomato, I could hardly complain, And Beena had done her best to make the tomato resemble a fried egg. Fortunately, we still had a good supply of my favourite pickles—garlic, mango, sweet lime, among others—and I went through all three toasts and a cup of tea without complaining. The tomato on toast wasn't bad. You should try it sometime.

10 April 2020

New day.
  Last night I had a dream. Or rather, early this morning I had a dream, which left me rather disturbed.

In my dream I was quite broke (as in former times) without any prospect of cheques and remittances from publishers, but I go to my bank anyway and ask the cashier to let me know the balance in my account. 'Two hundred rupees,' he says, looking sorry for me.

Still dreaming, I wander about in Dehradun. Old shopping centres are crumbling; new shopping centres look old and shabby. No customers in them. And I don't have enough money for a good meal.

Finally, I find a job on an ocean liner (and that too in landlocked Dehra) as a purser wearing a smart white uniform. Lots of money passes through my hands. The ship's captain (looking like Joseph Conrad) asks to see my poems.

End of the dream, as I remember it.

I have not attempted to interpret my dreams (although I record them from time to time), and I hope this doesn't indicate hard times for dear old Dehra, where I grew up. And I certainly wouldn't care to sail away on an ocean liner, especially now that most of them are saddled with coronavirus cases. And I can't imagine anyone wanting to see my poems.

Last year, I tried reading Freud's *The Interpretation of Dreams*, but found it tedious and unconvincing. Beena's homeopath, Dr Atul, does a better job of it. At least once a week she's on the phone talking to him, recounting her latest dream, and he responds with advice and his own interpretations, and she is apparently quickly satisfied with all of it. Dr Atul is a gentle person with a comforting manner, and he has a very large clientele.

⁓

Talking of dreams, I am reminded of Lincoln's dream on the night before his murder. It has often been told.

According to Attorney General Edward Bates, 'When we entered the Council Chambers today, we found the President seated at the top of the table with his face buried in his hands. Presently he raised his head, and we saw that he looked grave and worn. He said, "Gentlemen, before long, you will have important news." "Is it anything serious?" we enquired. "I have had a dream," he said. "I have dreamt that dream three times—once before the Battle of Bull Run, once on another occasion, and again last night. I am in a boat, alone—on a boundless ocean. I have no oars—no rudder—I am helpless, I drift! I drift!...."'

Five hours later, Lincoln was assassinated.

Do we drift today? Is the boat without a rudder, the world without a leader?

Trump is no Lincoln; not an idealist, nor a dreamer. His country has already lost over 20,000 souls to the virus. It drifts.... But he is counting dollars lost, not souls lost.

We are doing better here. But is the worst over, or is this only the beginning?

14 April 2020

The PM extends the lockdown till 3 May. That means nothing published, and no money coming in for several weeks. Fortunately, we have something in the bank, and the bank is on top of the hill, and it's usually open! But publishers' offices in Delhi remain closed. Most of them worked from home, anyway—but not the accountants!

Well, I've been working from home all my writing life, so this is simply an extension of my daily routine. But it's hard on young people, who like to go out, and it's hard on the millions of migrant labourers who are now in limbo all over the country—can't get work and can't go home.

I am now getting the newspaper, and I notice that the HT Classifieds, which would take up a page, has only one employment ad. If you're a radiologist, there's a job for you in Khanpur, Delhi.

Statistics. As of last evening, India has 9,431 confirmed cases, 335 deaths. About 1,000 have recovered, which is encouraging. Globally, there have been 2 million cases, over 115,000 deaths. Not so encouraging.

Yesterday, two mild earthquake tremors felt in Delhi and parts of our state, added a little excitement to the boredom of the lockdown. A real jolt would send everyone into the streets, and never mind the social distancing.

⌢

This would be an ideal time for stamp collecting, if stamp collecting hadn't gone out of fashion. I remember my father coming home from work and going straight to the cupboard where he kept his precious albums, catalogues, and the rest of the paraphernalia that went with his hobby. He specialized with the stamps of certain countries (Greece, Newfoundland, East Africa, the Solomon Islands!) and had separate albums for each one of them. He built up sets (according to their dates of use) and mounted them lovingly in those beautiful albums. I would help him with the sorting and built up a small collection of my own with his extras and rejects. When he died, I was at boarding school, and his valuable collection disappeared, probably looted by relations.

Discouraged, I gave up collecting, and gave my modest collection to a class fellow called MacDonald. He wasn't a close friend, but he was an avid collector, and I knew he would take care of the collection.

As a young man, when my father was working on a tea estate in Munnar (Travancore–Cochin in those days) he collected butterflies, and had a fine collection which he gave away to a museum where they could be better preserved.

I look out of my window and see a number of common cabbage white butterflies flittering about on the hillside. That means summer is here. It's getting really hot in the plains. Perhaps a hot, long summer will drive the virus away—fry it to a crisp and send it packing!

I must not forget to mention that we are getting eggs again, and that there was a fried egg on my toast this morning. It seemed bigger than usual. Hope it was a hen's!

Now I'm missing the fried tomato.

'Can't I have both, Beena?' I plead.

'Don't be greedy,' she says, but I get the tomato too.

The lockdown is not without its benefits!

16 April 2020

Skipped yesterday for various reasons. There was no TV till late in the evening, and then the usual statistics. Not a single advertisement in the newspaper, which just shows how businesses have been affected. I dreamt that Mr Mehra (my publisher at Rupa) had opened a chicken farm on his Dehradun property. There were smart cages, occupied by Disney-like hens all over the place. He offered me a job, collecting eggs as they were laid.

The Mehras are vegetarians, so I doubt they will switch from publishing books to raising chickens. I can supply them with stories but not eggs.

Although Mr Mehra doesn't eat eggs, he makes great omelettes, as I recall from the time I sometimes stayed with them, several years ago. That's probably the origin of the dream. And recently, I was dipping into Wodehouse's *Love Among the Chickens*; this was the first of his books that I read as a boy. Ukridge is probably my favourite character; always broke, but always on the verge of making a fortune.

Meanwhile, the ghost virus continues to infiltrate communities across the globe. It's like a ball of tumbleweed, flitting from one place to another—a will-o'-the-wisp—alighting randomly and without discrimination, taking some with it and discarding others, knowing it can't be stopped by the pompous men who run the world's affairs. Truly a ghost! You can't see it, you can't feel it, but it's there!

Unlike the Pied Piper, it doesn't take the children away. It seems to shy away from the innocent.

∽

Where does the virus come from?
From bats and dogs,
Or cats and frogs,
Or fallen logs,
And slimy bogs,
So where does the virus come from?

When will it come and when will it go?
It gives no warning and nobody knows.
It travels wherever it cares to roam,
And only the children are left alone.

Does it fear the children?
Nobody knows.

And so to bed (as Pepys once said).

17 April 2020

Up early, but no sunshine. Extensive cloud cover, promising rain. No birds sing. It would be depressing but for my window. For forty years (almost exactly) it has been my window on the world, except on those occasions when I have ventured into other parts of the land.

The view is the same, but no day is ever the same. The light changes, the air changes, the wind changes direction, the colour of the hillside changes, the trees come into new leaf or abandon old leaves.... The road below is usually quite busy with traffic, but since the lockdown it has been as quiet and as still has it must have been a hundred years ago, before the first motor car came up the hill.

There are two roads below me, connected by a footpath, and the lower one goes past 'Happy Bazaar' (so named in my last story)—the old Tehri bus stop—past Woodstock School, and then along the mountain range to Chamba and the Tehri dam. About forty miles of not very strenuous walking. When I was twenty, and a great walker, I walked to Chamba with a friend. We thought we'd get food along the way, but there wasn't any, except for some hard antiquated buns in a wayside teashop. From Chamba the road was motorable, and we took the bus down to Rishikesh and then to Dehradun (where

I was living at the time), and there we gorged ourselves on roast chicken and mutton chops. After that, I never went on a trek without an adequate supply of food. Now, at eighty-five, I find mutton chops a little hard on my teeth; but then, I don't walk to Chamba any more.

Newsbreak:
    Lockdown extended to 3 May.
    13,000 cases in India, 430 fatalities.
    2,100,000 cases globally, 136,000 fatalities.
Good news: No new cases in Uttarakhand (our state) for the third consecutive day. Something to be said for the mountains. And maybe the virus dislikes high altitudes.

To return to my window—and the monkey who has been sitting there for the last five minutes, looking rather forlorn. I give it a biscuit which it accepts. Usually, it just snatches the biscuit and makes off, leaping from the window ledge on to the lamp post. Today, it remains sitting at my window ledge. Perhaps, it's feeling lonely. It's used to seeing a lot of humans around, not all of them friendly. But the road below is empty. No one in sight. Where are all the people? It's over an hour since a vehicle passed this way, and then it was the garbage van.

Move to my little sunroom, to spend some time among my geraniums. Meditation, contemplation, cogitation, you can have it all in a garden or in the company of plants.

Give a plant time, protection, and the right nourishment, and it will reward you with flowers, fruit, foliage, colour, scent, shade, serenity. Why don't we go to them more often? We are too busy pushing them aside to make way for blocks and towns of concrete—and into those we scurry and hide when a virus gets out of hand. We play games with the natural order of things; now nature plays games with us.

Calm among the geraniums. Bright post-box red. A flood of tranquil pink. A deeper pink, sensual, beckoning. A crown of creamy white. So many shades, so many colours. And they speak to me, because I have watched over them and seen them grow. They are family.

I have watched children grow. I watched Rakesh grow. I watched his children grow. And they have responded, giving me love, affection, their very presence. No man is an island. Or is every man an island? Do we, in the end, have to live within ourselves and make our own peace with the universe?

No two people are the same. I can sit for an hour among the geraniums. I don't see the children spending a minute among them! They are hundreds, thousands of miles away, communicating with unseen friends on the little phones which are constant companions. You can get almost anything on them—news, entertainment, information, sight and sound—but not the human touch, not the kiss of love or passion, not the longing for something lost, not the gentle touch of the breeze, not the warmth of the sun or the birdsong at daybreak.

Here they come! A flock of parrots, flashes of green and red and gold. They swoop down to the oaks, feasting on acorns. Next month they will all be down in the valley, feasting on someone's mangoes. A parrot on a mango tree. There's freedom for you!

19 April 2020

Inevitably, one is drawn to the TV set, to be updated on the pandemic and how the virus is treating the human race; for it seems to be concentrating all its energies on people in preference to quadrupeds, winged creatures, birds, insects, and snails. And I have yet to hear of the virus being found in a fish. Although you never know. The scientists and medical experts come up with new theories every day. Some predict that it will all be over by June or July, latest. I hope coronavirus is listening.

TV is best watched in the morning. Seen last thing at night it is guaranteed to give you nightmares. This was so even before the virus came on the scene. As I have mentioned earlier, I found it difficult to sleep when haunted by images of starving children in Syria, or someone being lynched in our own country, or a psychopath in the USA gunning down people at random. I turned to the movie channels, but they too were full of scenes of torture and extreme violence, featuring madmen, aliens, anacondas, chemical weapons, viruses! After seeing hungry crocodiles feasting on scantily-clad bathers, I turned to our news channels, only to find TV debaters and their hosts snapping at each other like—like angry crocodiles! I tried the sports channels. Hunks of human flesh were busy flinging each other about, doing as much damage as possible to arms, legs, necks, and torsos.

'It's all play-acting,' says Gautam. 'They don't really hurt each other.'

I take his word for it. Try the cricket. The players don't sport beards. Oh, it's an old game, played in 1986. I recognize one of the players.

'Look, there's Mohinder Amarnath!' I exclaim.

Gautam looks blank. He wasn't born then.

Never mind. There's only one thing to do. Turn off the TV and read some poetry.

Poetry will always give you a good night's sleep. Sweet dreams, no nightmares. Keep an anthology of great poetry on your bedside table, and dip into it before switching off the light. This late hour is the best time for poetry; a time to remind oneself that there is still beauty in the world, and that sleep comes gently when we look for the beautiful in thought and words.

I go to my window and look out into the night. The moon is coming on over Landour, and a deodar on the summit of the mountain stands out in silhouette. Far down in the valley, the lights of Dehradun twinkle up at me. They are brighter than usual, partly due to last night's rain and partly due to the absence of pollution (the roads are empty, dark, and still!). Instead of car horns, I hear an owl hoot on a distant deodar.

21 April 2020

Statistics:
India   17,656 Covid-19 cases
           2,842 cured
           559 died
Worldwide 2,333,941

The US is the worst hit, with up to 40,661 deaths, due to largely haphazard measures and a haphazard president.

Let's move on to nicer things.

Shubhadarshini sends me enough chocolates to last until Christmas.

Saw an old Laurel & Hardy clip on Gautam's cell phone. Startled everyone with my laughter.

No cases in Mussoorie. At least none we know about (a few in Dehradun).

Working from home—I've been doing it for most of my adult life—that makes this easy.... But publishers are working from home too, which means no royalties until their offices reopen! If they reopen....

22 April 2020

Earth Day. Poor old earth. It has received a drubbing in recent years, especially from humankind. Homilies from all and sundry, but no one is really listening. Nature gives, and takes away, and gives again, but mankind can only take.

23 April 2020

Book day. Another forgotten day.
We take our books for granted, but a world without books would be like a world without grass. Just sand everywhere, and not even an earthworm beneath the surface.

Millions and millions of earthworms are tilling the soil on which we grow our grasses—wheat, maize, barley, rice, sugar cane, bamboo. Without them our fields would be fallow. Remember that the next time you shudder at the sight of an earthworm.

No butterflies today. A van has just driven past, pumping disinfectant into the air. The Mullinga's flat is barely visible. Even the monkeys have fled. Not a bird to be seen. They might kill the virus if they finish off everything else first!

24 April 2020

So where are all the people? My dreams are full of them. I dream of crowds and crowded places—railway stations, fairgrounds, benches, football stadiums, shopping malls, riverfronts....

In last night's dream I was a circus clown, and everyone was kissing me—the pretty South Indian trapeze artist, the dancing ponies, the tightrope walker, the ringmaster, the bearded lady!

As the bearded lady hovered over me, I woke up.

I used to enjoy going to the circus when I was a boy. The circus tents would come up on Dehra's parade ground, and for a week or two, they would be crowded with an enthusiastic public. No TV then. The performance included animals—lions, tigers, ponies, even elephants. Now, without the animals, the circuses aren't much fun, and there are only one or two left in the country.

Long ago, I met a girl who used to walk the tightrope. She spoke and wrote good English (unlike most circus artistes) and for several years she corresponded with me from different parts of the country. Then she emigrated to Australia and I did not hear from her again. Survival is a balancing act for most of us.

Phyllis Bottome (a good writer, now forgotten) once wrote a short story about a lion and a lion tamer who had a very close and affectionate relationship. Every night the lion tamer would end their act by placing his head in the lion's mouth. Then one night the lion felt sleepy—or just plain bored—yawned and shut his mouth with a snap, and off went his friend's head.

∽

A phone call from Chand (in Dehra) to tell me that he is just out of hospital after recovering from the coronavirus infection. Chand is about my age, maybe a year or two younger. We first met in 1950, when I was down from school for my winter holidays. He was a good badminton player, and that's how we met. There were Chand and Bhim, and Ranbir and his sister Raj, and we would play badminton in the evenings, towards the end of March, when the air was full of the fragrance of mango blossom. It was an outdoor court, behind the station canteen. Raj was a lovely girl; not pretty, but vivacious. She had sparkly eyes and a flashing smile. I wasn't much of a badminton player, but I enjoyed her company and was really quite smitten by her. She would beat me 21–0, 21–2, or something like that; but I did not mind, I just wanted to be with her. It was truly a love game. When I went to England, I lost touch with her. And, when I returned, it was to find that she and Ranbir had left Dehra. But Chand was still around, and still is ringing me up from time to time. And surviving the coronavirus.

Badminton in the mango grove. Those were the days, my

friend, we thought they'd never end.... And it's wonderful to have a good memory.

Store up your memories, for they'll give you company on cold winter nights.

26 April 2020

I've been doing readings of some of my stories for All India Radio (AIR), courtesy Ms Banerjee, who did an interview with me a few years ago. I read into the telephone (the landline)—four ten-minute stories during the last two days, and two for tomorrow. She seemed quite happy with the result, and I enjoyed doing it.

When I was in London (1953–54), I gave a couple of talks for the BBC Home Service. My producer, a kind lady called Prudence Smith, first gave me some lessons in elocution, in order to tone down my strong sing-song accent. Later, a number of my stories were broadcast in their fifteen-minute short story slot—stories such as 'The Night Train at Deoli', 'The Thief', 'The Woman on Platform 8', 'The Eyes Have It', etc.,—stories that are still around today...so I owe something to those 'radio days', and it's nice to be working with radio again.

Better to be heard than to be seen!

∽

I have kept a diary, or journal, off and on throughout my life, and apart from giving me pleasure, it has been the bedrock of much of my writing. My first novel grew out of my diary, so did many stories—although they'd become fiction in the process.

A journal that was, in fact, fiction, was Daniel Defoe's *A Journal of the Plague Year*, although he based it very closely on factual accounts. He was adept at that sort of thing. *Robinson Crusoe* was based on the experiences of a shipwrecked sailor, Alexander Selkirk; and *Moll Flanders* was a realistic account of the life of a London prostitute.

I found John Evelyn's diaries rather tedious, but James Boswell's *London Journal* is most entertaining and revealing; and, of course, Pepys was the master diarist, informative, observant, witty, and full of his many flirtations.

A number of famous people have kept diaries which were hurriedly destroyed by their heirs soon after their demise. Kipling's private papers were burnt by his widow; Sir Richard Burton's letters and journals met a similar fate.

Sometimes we are wise to do away with our own private scribblings. My school diary fell into the hands of my class master and got me into trouble; my observations on his wife were not appreciated.

If you keep a diary, don't leave it lying around. Remember—when you keep a diary you are talking to yourself, not to others—and your private thoughts may not go down well with someone who comes across them by chance or design.

When I was in the UK, living with relatives (I was seventeen at the time) I made an entry in my diary to the effect that I was sick and tired of living with relatives! My uncle read the entry and naturally there was an unpleasant scene. A week later, I left his house and went to London and lived on my own for two years and became a writer of sorts. So, the outcome was a good one, in the end. Frank Swinnerton spoke truly when he wrote: 'There are neither rewards nor punishments in life. There are just consequences.'

'And so to bed' (as Pepys said)....

Respect Your Bed

In bed we lie, in bed we sleep,
In bed we laugh, in bed we weep,
In bed we groan when racked with pain,
And when we're well we smile again.
In bed we toss, in bed we snore,
We wake up late, then sleep some more.
In bed we scratch, in bed we curse
If bugs abound, or something worse!
In bed we dream, in bed we mope,
We sigh but never give up hope.
In bed we're born, in bed we die
Unless of course we climb a peak
And from it fall a thousand feet!
Most of one's life is spent in bed
A horizontal human, better than
Standing still with unsupported head
Respect your bed, my friend
It's there beside you till the end.
So keep it soft, and keep it neat,
And may God bless your tired feet.

Come to think of it, I've been using the same old wooden bed for close to fifty years, and in this time, I've put on quite a bit of weight. But it has put up with the overload very sportingly, although it does occasionally give a groan or a moan of protest when I come down on it too heavily.

I have always made my own bed, ever since my school days, and I have some difficulty in sleeping in strange beds—especially hotel beds. The more elaborate the bed, the harder it is to manage. The sheets are usually jammed beneath the mattress in such a way that it takes a herculean effort to free them. Several pillows are stacked up at the head of the bed, and have to be flung away, one by one, through the long sleepless hours of the night, until you are down to one pillow.

Never sleep with more than one soft pillow. If you go through life sleeping with a mountain of pillows, you'll end up a hunchback.

Some simple rules for a happy life:

- Make your own bed.
- Use it as often as possible.
- Don't watch TV before going to bed—read some poetry instead.
- Sleep with only one pillow.
- Keep an extra pillow just in case you wish to share your bed with someone very nice (such as your spouse).

29 April 2020

> Cases in India 30,000
> Fatalities 1,000
> Recoveries 7,000
> Better than most countries but lockdown continues....

A depressing morning, with a heavy mist cutting us off from the world.

I think it was Thomas Hardy who espoused the view that God created a beautiful world and then forgot all about it, leaving us to the vagaries of chance and (to a limited extent) our own ingenuity.

I have been writing for seventy years, and yet it all seems so evanescent, so fleeting, so trivial. Still, it did sustain me (and two generations of my chosen family) for the better part of my life, in spite of many setbacks and failures.

How important it is to experience failure, not once but again and again, and, more important still, to recover from it. If you don't recover, you're finished.

The most difficult failure is that in which you come down from a 'high'—reach the peak or summit of your profession, of all your achievements, and then find yourself plunging downwards, with no one or nothing to sustain you—except, perhaps, alcohol, in the case of writers such as Scott Fitzgerald, Hemingway, Dylan Thomas, Jack London, the list is a long one; and the list of actors, singers, performers, who have succumbed to the pressures of success is even longer.

I was lucky to have had a small success when I was still very young (but I worked very hard for it), followed by a series of flops—these failures preparing me for a literary life which was a sequence of ups and downs. After *The Room on the Roof*, I couldn't get anyone to publish my longer works; so I concentrated on the short stuff, became a storyteller instead of a novelist, and had no significant problems after that.

And that's what I tell every young aspiring writer. Find out what you're good at, and stick to it. Don't try to be Hemingway. Even he couldn't live up to the image he'd built of himself. Be yourself. And be honest with yourself.

Some lines from Shakespeare that my father quoted in my autograph book when I was a small boy:

> This above all, to thy own self be true,
> And it must follow, as the night the day,
> Thou canst not then be false to any man.

3 May 2020

Last day of Lockdown 2.
Lockdown 3 starts tomorrow, but many restrictions lifted. Cases and fatalities increase all over the world, but rich people are losing money and poor people their livelihoods, so most governments are in retreat.

The cold, wet spell continues, and the parrots have gone elsewhere.

All India Radio (AIR) wants me to read more stories, and I am happy to do so. Hope someone is listening to them!

India is a musical country, and singing under lockdown has become a national pastime. It is even recommended by doctors. Italy is also a musical country, and we are constantly being shown some snippets of sopranos and baritones belting out operatic arias from their balconies. It takes me back to my childhood and the old gramophone, on which Gigli, the great tenor, would rend the sultry air of Jamnagar with his rendering of that tender aria from *La Boheme*, 'Che gehda manina'

I wish I had been an opera singer, but friends and family forbid me from singing where others can hear me. According to them, when I hit a low note, I sound like a bullfrog being strangled by a snake, and when I hit a high note I sound like a dinosaur in distress. I correct them all now. It should be more like a dinosaur singing. If frogs could sing, so could dinosaurs. If Caruso could sing, so can I.

Our music teacher at school, Mrs Whitmarsh Knight, tried to stop me. She put me in the school choir because she thought I looked 'sweet' in a cassock and surplice, and she told me to open and shut my mouth with the others in the choir but on no account to permit any sound from issuing forth. I went through this pantomime at every rehearsal, and then, when the big day arrived and we put on Handel's *Messiah* in the school chapel, I couldn't resist joining in with the 'Hallelujah!' chorus, and this brought the entire performance to a halt. There was a dead silence, and in that silence I piped up with another 'Hallelujah!' of my own, and was banished from the choir forever. Poor Mrs Knight. It was several months before she recovered from her nervous breakdown.

9 May 2020

Last night the moon was red. Blood red, and surrounded by a reddish halo. It was at the full and from my window we watched it come up over the mountain.

Beena said a red moon foretold disaster, but we already have plenty of that. Will things get worse?

Gautam said it was red because Trump had started mining on the moon (as promised). I said he was probably laying out a golf course, so that he could spend his retirement up there.

Meanwhile, his country and Britain and others are being ravaged by the coronavirus, and all the king's scientists and all the king's men are unable to do anything about it. And all the economists give varying predictions. What do economists really do, apart from picking up Nobel prizes? They don't seem to agree on anything.

The red moon kept staring at me through my window, preventing me from sleeping. Finally, I dozed off and dreamt that I was waylaid by thieves while walking down to the town. A kind passer-by dealt with one of them, and I dealt with the other by clobbering him on the hand with the book I was holding. The thieves fled. I recall the title of the book. It was *The Consolation of Philosophy* in a sturdy binding. I've had it for years, and have often tried reading it, but I doze off after a page or two. Must try again, now that it's part of my defensive armour.

11 May 2020

I notice a slight improvement of my vision—without glasses. Or maybe it's just that the sky is clearer these days.

And here comes the sun, after two or three cloudy and thundery mornings. A hawk circles overhead. There are children at the water tap. A man walks his dog. We are open till noon. Hard to believe that in the rest of the country there are now some 60,000 cases of the virus, with over 2,000 fatalities; 4 million worldwide, with over a million in America, the world's most powerful nation, with the UK not far behind, and then Russia! The world's great powers no longer invincible. The virus is an unguided missile.

The roads beyond the district are still closed, so Rakesh and Beena have to put off their annual pilgrimage to Badrinath. But we are lucky to be here in Landour. Will the tourists start pouring in, once the lockdown is over? It will take some time but come back they will. And the litter will be back on the roads. Human nature doesn't change.

14 May 2020

Panic in Landour. Someone who returned from Delhi fell ill and tested positive for the virus. The sub-divisional magistrate (SDM) has had the bazaar shut down. Before that, everyone was running about buying vegetables and other provisions, not knowing when the markets would reopen. There was also a rush on the liquor shop, as the liquor vendors have announced a strike from tomorrow, in protest against an exorbitant 'health tax'.

Gave my fifteenth (and final) story reading for AIR, under the guidance of the enthusiastic and ebullient Ms Banerjee in her home in New Delhi—all done courtesy my old-fashioned landline telephone! This gave me some pleasure during this lockdown, and I am told that it has given pleasure to many listeners, children and parents, here and abroad. Happiness is an elusive thing, to be found somewhere between too little and too much.

16 May 2020

Statistics are beginning to scare me, so I won't dwell on them, except to note that at 85,000 cases we have now gone past China and are in hot pursuit of Trumpland, though without as many casualties.

As restrictions are lifted (as they must be), the infection spreads (as it must) and many are now reluctant to emerge from the safety of their homes. Maybe humankind is destined to once again become a race of cave dwellers. Ironically, that's where bats live, too!

The saddest sights (on TV) are of hundreds, thousands of migrant workers with women and children, trudging homewards, often for distances of hundreds of miles. At first, they were prevented from leaving the cities where they were thrown out of work; and then, after languishing for weeks, they were told they could go, but only limited transport was provided. Many have perished on the way. Will they return to the cities if needed again (as they will be)? Only if circumstances compel them to do so.

While on the subject of bats, supposedly the origins of the virus, I remember my mother telling me a story about a relative, a cousin of hers, who, when pregnant, was terrified by a colony of bats that had taken up residence under the roof beams of her house. When the baby was born, he was found to have webbed fingers, like a bat's wings.

When I told this story to Gautam he said, 'With those hands he should have become a great swimmer!'

I'm told that there's an Olympic swimmer with webbed feet. Perhaps his mother was frightened by a duck.

17 May 2020

Up at 5 a.m. There was a half-moon riding the sky in the east, and below it the flow of the early dawn as it spread behind the mountains. Sun, moon, and sky in a happy conjunction.

Only a human has the intelligence and sensitivity to be able to appreciate the wonder of nature; and it is only humans who are capable of degrading and destroying the natural world, and who do so wilfully. Degrees of intelligence? Some are born with it; some are born idiots.

18 May 2020

Lockdown 4 begins. No let-up in the spread of the virus.

Books that I have read more than once over the years:

- *The Story of my Heart* by Richard Jefferies
- *Alice in Wonderland* by Lewis Carroll
- *The Diary of a Nobody* by George and Weedon Grossmith
- *Wuthering Heights* by Emily Bronte
- *Typhoon* by Joseph Conrad (long short story)
- *The Bird of Dawning* by John Masefield
- *Fruits of the Earth* by André Gide
- *The Quest for Corvo* by A. J. A. Symons
- *The House of the Arrow* by A. E. W. Mason
- *Seven Men* by Max Beerbohm

19 May 2020

Have completed eighty-six years on Planet Earth.
Up with the lark (or rather, the monkey on the roof) and surveyed the landscape from my window: the sun coming up over Pari Tibba, then spreading across the valley.

Rakesh and Beena come to wish me a happy birthday. They have cared for me so beautifully all these years. Prem, Rakesh's father, before them. Time gives us the slip.... And suddenly the world is old.

I shall close this portion of my journal today, as there are other stories to write. This morning's quote in the *Times of India* says it all:

> Of course, some people want literature to be difficult and there are writers who like to make their readers toil and sweat. They hope to be taken more seriously that way. I have always tried to achieve a prose that is easy and conversational.

(Interesting, to come across a quote of one's own. I shall endeavour to live up to it!)

Every day is a birthday. For you and me and the monkey on the roof.

Happy birthday, world!